kids' knitted
sweaters & more

Knitting sweaters for children is fun and fast. To make it more rewarding and even more fun, we have eliminated the need to sew the pieces of your sweater together. Most of the designs in this book are knit in one piece! We show you examples of knitting construction from three different directions. Choose one of the cozy pullovers knit in the round from the bottom up or from the top down. Or choose a cardigan or vest made in one piece, working back and forth on a circular needle. These can also be knitted from the top down with no seams to sew. For something different, work one sweater from each of the cuffs then join in the middle.

In these designs, Deb, Lynda, and fellow Cabin Fever designers Dana Gibbons, Mary K Hobbs, Megan Lacey, Karen Lawrence, Cynthia MacDougall, Anne Russell, Bernice Vollick, and Shirl the Purl have followed the Cabin Fever creed of minimal finishing. So grab your circular needles and enjoy creating amazing sweaters your little ones will love to wear.

Deb & Lynda Gemmell
Cabin Fever

designers

Cabin Fever is a design company created by sisters Deb and Lynda Gemmell to feed their knitting habit. From an idea hatched on the deck of their cabin in Northern Ontario over several summers, Cabin Fever has grown into the largest independent knitting pattern publisher in Canada.

We welcome your comments and suggestions.

Please email, fax or phone us at:

Cabin Fever

Orillia, Ontario, Canada

Phone: 800-671-9112;

705-326-1900 (Canada)

Fax: 705-326-9956

Website: www.cabinfever.ca

Email: info@cabinfever.ca

Produced for Leisure Arts by Kooler Design Studio, Inc.
Kooler Design Studio office:
399 Taylor Blvd., Ste. 104
Pleasant Hill, CA 94523
Contact: info@koolerdesign.com
Website: www.koolerdesign.com

Production Team
Creative Director: Donna Kooler
Editor-In-Chief: Judy Swager
Technical Editor: Marsha Hinkson
Book Designer/Illustrator: María Rodríguez
Writers: Cabin Fever Designers
Photographer: Dianne Woods
Photo Stylist: Basha Kooler
Proofreader: Char Randolph

International Standard Book Number: 1-57486-609-5

Published by

contents

knitting **basics**

terms

I-Cord – See techniques on page 5 for explanation.

K2tog – Knit 2 stitches together.

Kfb – Knit into front and back of same stitch: Increase of 1 stitch by knitting into front of next stitch and without removing stitch, knit into back of same stitch.

knitwise or kwise – Insert needle into stitch as if to knit.

m – meter

M1 – Make 1 stitch. With left needle, lift the running thread between the stitch just worked and the next stitch, from front to back, and knit into the back of the resulting loop.

M1(k) – Make 1 stitch (no hole) knitwise. With the left needle lift the running thread between the stitch just worked and the next stitch, from front to back, and knit into the back of the resulting loop.

M1(p) – Make 1 stitch (no hole) purlwise. With the left needle lift the running thread between the stitch just worked and the next stitch, from back to front, and purl into the front of the resulting loop.

Purlwise or Pwise – Insert needle into stitch as if to purl.

Shapeline – The stitch (or stitches) separating the pair of increases creating the distinctive diagonal line of the raglan yoke.

SL1 – Transfer 1 stitch from left needle to right needle without working it.

SL(k) – Slip stitch knitwise: Transfer stitch from left needle to right needle without working it by inserting right needle into stitch as if you were about to knit the stitch; slide stitch off left needle onto right needle.

SL1(p) – Slip stitch purlwise with yarn in back. Transfer stitch from left needle to right needle without working it by inserting right needle into stitch as if you were about to purl the stitch; slide stitch off left needle onto right needle.

SL2(k)-K1-P2SSO – With right needle, slip 2 stitches together knitwise, knit next stitch, pass the 2 slipped stitches over the knit stitch and off the end of right needle.

SSK – Slip, Slip, Knit: Slip first stitch as if to knit, slip next stitch as if to knit, insert left needle into fronts of 2 slipped stitches on right needle and knit 2 stitches together.

YO – Yarn over: Bring yarn under right needle to front of work, then swing yarn over right needle to back of work — ready to work next stitch.

YRN – Yarn around needle: Bring yarn over and back to front again of right needle — ready to purl next stitch.

knit terminology

United States	International
gauge = tension	
bind off = cast off	
yarn over (YO) = yarn forward (yfwd) **or**	
	yarn around needle (yrn)

special stitches

Knit 2 stitches together (K2tog): Insert the right needle into the front of the second, then the first stitch on the left needle as if to knit (fig. 1) and knit them together as if they were one stitch. This decrease slants to the right and is one of the most frequently used.

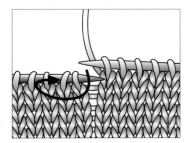

fig. 1

Make 1 (M1): Insert the left needle under the horizontal strand between the stitches from the front (fig. 2a). Then knit into the back of the strand (fig. 2b).

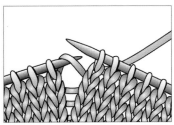

fig. 2a   fig. 2b

abbreviations

CC	contrasting color
cm	centimeter(s)
g	gram
k or K	knit
k2tog	knit 2 stitches together
kwise	knitwise
lp(s)	loop(s)
m	meter(s)
M1	make one—an increase—several increases can be described as "M1"
MC	Main Color
mm	millimeters
pat(s) or patt	pattern(s)
p2tog	purl 2 stitches together
psso	pass slipped stitch over
pwise	purlwise
rnd(s)	round(s)
RS	right side
sl	slip
sl1k	slip 1 knitwise
sl1p	slip 1 purlwise
ssk	slip, slip, knit these 2 stitches together —a decrease
sssk	slip, slip, slip, knit 3 stitches together
st(s)	stitch(es)
St st	stockinette stitch/stocking stitch
tog	together
WS	wrong side
yd(s)	yard(s)

3

Slip, Slip, Knit (SSK): Slip the first stitch as if to knit, then slip the next stitch as if to knit (fig. 3a). Insert the left needle into the front of both slipped stitches (fig. 3b) and knit them together (fig. 3c). This decrease also slants to the left and is interchangeable with slip 1, K1, PSSO. However, because SSK is the mirror image of K2tog, it is often used when the decreases will be visible, as in raglan sleeve sweaters.

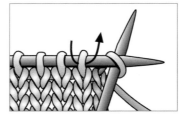

fig. 3a

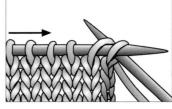

fig. 3b

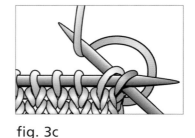

fig. 3c

techniques

Knitting in the Round

Using a circular needle, cast on all stitches as instructed. Untwist and straighten on the needle before beginning the first round. Place a marker after the last stitch to mark the beginning of a round. Hold the needle so that the ball of yarn is attached to the stitch closest to the right hand point. To begin working in the round, knit the stitches on the left hand point (fig. 4).

Continue working each round as instructed without turning the work. After the first round, check to be sure that the cast on edge has not been twisted. If it has been, the only way to correct the twist is to rip out the first round back to the cast row. Join, being careful not to twist the cast on row, and work the first row again. Check again to ensure that the work has not been twisted.

When working a project that is too small to use a circular needle, or the size circular needle is unavailable in the length needed, double pointed needles are required. Divide the number of cast on stitches into

fig. 4

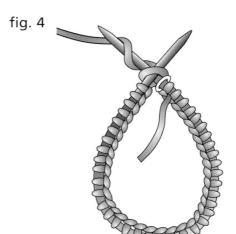

fig. 5a

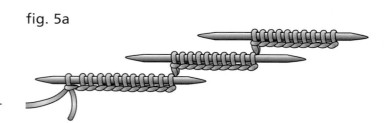

thirds or fourths and slip ⅓ or ¼ of the stitches onto each of the double pointed needles, forming a triangle or square. With the last needle, knit across the first needle (fig. 5a – 5b). You will now have an empty needle with which to knit the stitches from the next needle. Work the first stitch of each needle firmly to prevent gaps.

fig. 5b

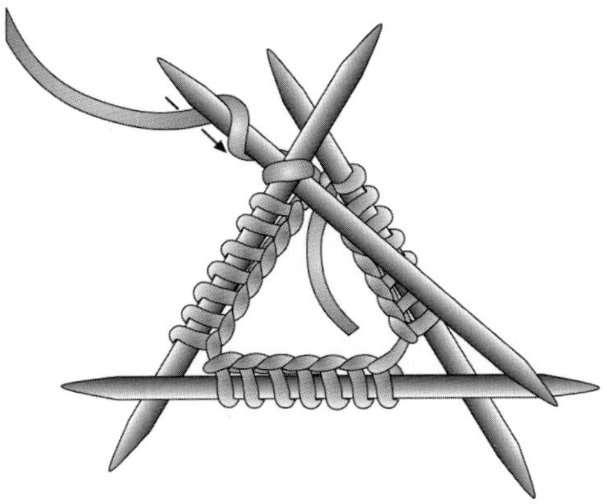

I-Cord

Using 2 double pointed needles, cast on 3 or more stitches (fig. 6a).

Knit every stitch. **DO NOT TURN** (fig. 6b).

Slide stitches to right end of needle. Pull yarn tightly across back of the stitches before knitting next row (fig. 6c).

Repeat steps 2 and 3 until I-cord measures desired length (fig. 6d).

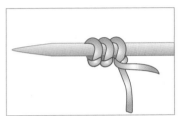

fig. 6a

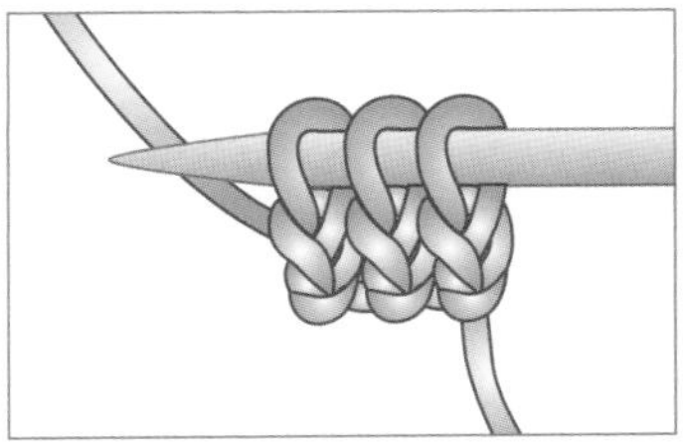

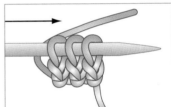

fig. 6b

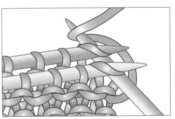

fig. 6c

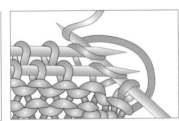

fig. 6d

3-Needle Bind Off

With RS of pieces facing, insert the left-hand needle as if to knit into the first stitch on the front needle and into the first stitch on the back needle. Knit these two stitches together and slip them off the needle (fig. 7a).

*Knit the next two stitches together same as above. You now have two stitches on right-hand needle (fig. 7b).

To bind off, insert the left needle into the first stitch on the right needle and lift the first stitch over the second stitch and off the needle. Repeat from * across until all of the stitches are bound off (fig. 7c).

fig. 7a

fig. 7b

fig. 7c

top down
sweaters

We love a construction method that means no seams and no sewing, so we're big fans of knitting from the top down! There are other advantages, too: you can try the sweater on the little tyke as you go to check for size, and adjust body and sleeve length on the fly. Then, as your young sweater owner grows, it's easy to pull off the cuffs and add length to the body and sleeves.

How is it done? Both cardigans and pullovers are started at the neck and worked down the body, then the sleeves are knit down to the wrists. Cardigans are worked back and forth, and collar and buttonbands can be made as you work the sweater — no need to do it later! Pullovers are knit around and around. With no specific front or back, the child can never put the sweater on backwards.

We've provided a range of sweaters knit from the top down, from a very easy first-time pullover, the Autumn Stripes, to the challenging Mariposa Blocks with seven colors worked across the yoke.

sophia's ridged
cardigan

I designed this cardigan to be easy to knit and quick to finish with no sewing except to attach the buttons. If I could figure out how to attach buttons without taking a threaded needle in hand, I would. That just may be the next challenge — stay tuned. This pattern is a cardigan, worked from the top down. Work yoke increases in a circle with eight increase lines. Each increase line consists of two stitches between the increases.

Style Notes: Knit from the top down with no sewing.

Designer: Bernice Vollick
Experience Level: Beginner

sizes
To fit Child: 1 (2, 4, 6) years

finished measurements
Chest: 24 (26, 29, 31)"
Body Length: 12 (13, 15, 17)"
Sleeve Length: 6½ (8, 10, 12)"

materials
DK, Light Worsted Weight yarn (3.5 ounces/
    250 yards, 100 grams/230 meters per ball):
        Pink 2 (2, 3, 3) balls
Size 6 (4.0 mm) 24" (60 cm) circular needle
Set of size 6 (4.0 mm) double pointed needles
8 markers
9 (10, 10, 13) ½-inch buttons
Stitch holders

gauge
22 stitches = 4" (10 cm) on size 6 (4.0 mm) needles or size needed to obtain gauge

collar

With circular needle cast on 64 (72, 76, 84) sts.
Work back and forth on circular needle:
Row 1: (RS) K3, work [P2, K2] to last stitch, K1.
Row 2: P3, work [K2, P2] to last stitch, P1.
Repeat last 2 rows until work measures 1 (1, 1½, 1½)"
from cast on edge, ending with Row 2.

yoke

Next Row: (RS) Knit, increasing 0 (1, 4, 5) sts evenly,
— 64 (73, 80, 89) sts on the needle.
In the following row place 8 markers for the increase
lines of the yoke:
Marker Row: (WS) P4 (5, 5, 6), place marker, *P8 (9,
10, 11) sts, place marker; repeat from * until 4 (5, 5,
6) sts remain, purl to end of row.

ridge pattern

Row 1 (Increase Row): (RS) *Knit to 1 stitch before
the marker, M1, K1, slip marker, K1, M1; repeat from

* 7 more times (just past last marker), knit to end of
row — 80 (89, 96, 105) sts.
Row 2: (WS) P3, *knit to 1 stitch before the marker,
P1, slip marker, P1; repeat from * 7 more times, knit
to last 3 sts, P3 (makes ridges on RS).
Row 3: (RS) Knit.
Row 4: (WS) Purl.
Repeat Rows 1–4 until there are 208 (233, 256, 265)
sts on needle, ending with Row 4.
You should have 13 (15, 16, 17) stitches between the
Front edge and first marker, 26 (29, 32, 33) sts
between each of the markers, and 13 (15, 16, 17) sts
between last marker and Front edge.

Next Row: (RS) Knit.
Next Row: (WS) Purl, removing 8 markers as you go.
Repeat last 2 rows, without any further increases, until
the yoke measures 6 (7, 7½, 8)", measured vertically
from the base of the collar to the needle, ending with
a WS row.

Divide for the sleeves and body: (RS) K31 (34, 37, 38) for the Left Front, thread the next 42 (48, 54, 56) sts onto a stitch holder or spare piece of yarn for the sleeves, knit the next 62 (69, 74, 77) sts for the Back, thread the next 42 (48, 54, 56) sts onto a stitch holder or spare piece of yarn for the second sleeve, K31 (34, 37, 38) for the Right Front — 124 (137, 148, 153) sts on the circular needle.

body

Continue to work in Stockinette Stitch (knit on RS, purl on WS) until work measures 4½ (4½, 5½, 7)" from underarm, ending with a WS row.

Decrease Row: (RS) Knit, decreasing 8 (9, 8, 9) sts evenly around the body — 116 (128, 140, 144) sts on circular needle.

Bottom Ribbing
Row 1: (WS) P3, work [K2, P2] to last stitch, P1.
Row 2: (RS) K3, work [P2, K2] to last stitch, K1.
Repeat last 2 rows until ribbed band measures 1½ (1½, 2, 2)", ending with a WS row.
Bind off in ribbing.

sleeves (worked in the round)

Set-Up Rnd: Distribute stitches from stitch holder or yarn evenly onto 3 double pointed needles. With RS facing, and starting at center of the underarm, use fourth needle to pick up and K1 stitch between Front and Back of the yoke. Knit around the sleeve stitches, keeping the stitches evenly distributed on the 3 double pointed needles, place marker for beginning of rnd — 43 (49, 55, 57) sts on the needles.

Rnds 1–7: Knit.
Rnd 8: K1, SSK, knit to last 2 sts of rnd, K2tog.
Repeat last 8 rnds, until sleeve measures 5 (6½, 8, 10)" from underarm. Do not decrease to less than 41 (41, 45, 45) sts.

cuff

Next Rnd: Knit, decreasing to 40 (40, 44, 44) sts.
Next Rnd: Work [K2, P2] to end of rnd.
Repeat last rnd until cuff measures 1½ (1½, 2, 2)".
Bind off in ribbing.

garter stitch buttonhole band (RF)

Set-Up Row: With RS facing, pick up and knit 67 (72, 82, 93) sts evenly along the Front edge of the sweater.
Rows 1–3: Knit — 2 Garter Stitch ridges show on the RS.
Row 4 (Buttonhole): (RS) K5 (4, 4, 4), *YO, K2tog, K5 (5, 6, 5); repeat from * to last 6 (5, 6, 5) sts, YO, K2tog, knit to end of row.
Row 5: (WS) Knit.
Row 6: (RS) Knit.
With WS facing, bind off knitwise.

garter stitch button band (LF)

Set-Up Row: With RS facing, pick up and knit 67 (72, 82, 93) sts evenly along the Front edge of the sweater.
Knit 6 rows, ending with a RS row.
With WS facing, bind off knitwise.

finishing

Weave in the ends, sew buttons in place.

mariposa **blocks**

The colors for this sweater were inspired by a set of building blocks. I chose two colorways that I thought would be appropriate for both boys and girls but you can go to town on color selection!

Style Notes: Work this garment from the top down. Use markers to indicate divisions between body segments. Slip these markers when they are encountered. Incorporate buttonholes into the button band as you work down the body of the sweater.

Designer: Cynthia MacDougall
Experience Level: Advanced

sizes
To fit Child: 1 (2, 4 , 6) years

finished measurements
Chest: 24 (26, 28, 30)"
Body Length: 12 (13, 14, 16)"
Sleeve Length: 6½ (8, 10, 12)"

materials
DK, Light Worsted Weight Yarn (4 ounces/
    250 yards, 125grams/230 meters per skein)
    1 skein each:
        Sweater 1: Teal (A), Orange (B), Green (C),
        Yellow (D), Blue (E)
        Sweater 2: Navy (A), Green (B), Red (C),
        Yellow (D), Blue (E)
Size 6 (4.0 mm) 24" (60 cm) circular needle or
    two straight needles
Set of size 6 (4.0 mm) double pointed needles
3–6 ½-inch buttons depending on finished length
4 markers
Yarn bobbins
Darning needle

gauge

22 sts and 30 rows = 4" (10 cm) on size 6 (4.0 mm) needle or size needed to obtain gauge

begin with garter stitch neckband

NOTE: Work the neckband in two pieces, starting at the Center Back of the neck. Work short rows (partial rows) on the outside edge, making the neckband curve in a shallow "C." Stitches will be picked up along the outside edge of the neckband to begin the body of the sweater.

First Half of Neckband

With 2 double pointed needles and A, cast on 5 (5, 7, 7) sts.
Knit 12 (16, 16, 24) rows. (With RS facing 6 [8, 8, 12] ridges show on RS of neckband.)

Rows 1 and 2 (Short Rows): K3 (3, 5, 5), turn, K3 (3, 5, 5) back to beginning of row. (With RS facing 1 partial ridge shows on outside edge.)
Rows 3–8: Knit. (With RS facing, 3 more ridges will show).

Repeat Rows 1–8, 2 (2, 3, 3) more times.
Repeat Short Rows 1 and 2, once more.
Knit 2 rows. (With RS facing you should see a total of 20 [22, 26, 30] ridges on outside edge where short rows were worked.)
Leave 5 (5, 7, 7) sts on one of the double pointed needles.

Second Half of Neckband

With 2 double pointed needles and A, cast on 5 (5, 7, 7) sts and work as for first half of neckband. Knit 1 more row on second half of neckband, ending at inside edge.

yoke

NOTE: Pick up yoke stitches and knit off of the 2 neckbands. The short rows (partial rows) on the outside edge of both halves of neckbands make them curve in a shallow "C." Pick up stitches along the outside edge (outside of "C") of the neckbands to begin the body of the sweater.

Colorways

*NOTE: You need to wind 3 bobbins of A (2 for 2 button bands, 1 for Back).

	*Teal	*Navy
Color A		
Color B	Orange	Green
Color C	Green	Red
Color D	Yellow	Yellow
Color E	Blue	Blue

In the next row you will pick up 1 stitch in each ridge of the outside edge of neckbands and place 4 raglan markers as follows:

Row 1: With circular needle, second neckband and A, K5 (5, 7, 7) sts off of double pointed needle of second neckband. Along outside edge of same neckband, pick up and knit 2 sts with B for Front. Place marker, pick up and knit 6 (8, 10, 12) sts with C for left sleeve. Place marker, pick up and knit 12 (12, 14, 16) sts with second bobbin of A to end of neckband at Center Back, starting at the cast on end of first neckband and continuing with A, pick up and knit along outside edge 12 (12, 14, 16) sts for Back. Place marker, pick up and knit 6 (8, 10, 12) sts with D for right sleeve, place marker, pick up and knit 2 sts with E for Front, with third bobbin of A, K5 (5, 7, 7) sts from double pointed needle — 50 (54, 66, 74) sts.

Working back and forth on circular needle:

Row 2: (WS) K5 (5, 7, 7) with A, bring A to front of work and twist colors, P2 with E, P6 (8, 10, 12) with D, P24 (24, 28, 32) with A, P6 (8, 10, 12) with C, P2 with B, twist colors and bring A to back and K5 (5, 7, 7) with A — 50 (54, 66, 74) sts.

Row 3: K5 (5, 7, 7) with A, K1, M1, K1 with B, K6 (8, 10, 12) with C, K24 (24, 28, 32) with A, K6 (8, 10, 12) with D, K1, M1, K1 with E, K5 (5, 7, 7) with A — 52 (56, 68, 76) sts.

Row 4: K5 (5, 7, 7) with A, P3 with E, P6 (8, 10, 12) with D, P24 (24, 28, 32) with A, P6 (8, 10, 12) with C, P3 with B, K5 (5, 7, 7) with A.

Work the following rows increasing before and after each of the raglan markers every other row as directed. **At the same time** increasing at the neck edge every 4th row, change colors as established and maintain the button bands in A:

Row 5: (RS) K5 (5, 7, 7) sts of button band, *knit to 1 stitch before marker, M1, K1, slip marker and change color, K1, M1; repeat from * at next 3 markers, knit to last 5 (5, 7, 7) sts, K5 (5, 7, 7) sts of button band. (Increase of 8 sts in row.)

Row 6: K5 (5, 7, 7) sts of button band, purl to last 5 (5, 7, 7) sts, changing colors as established, knit button band sts.

Row 7 (neck edge increase): (RS) K5 (5, 7, 7) for button band, in first color section, K1, M1, *knit to 1 stitch before marker, M1, K1, slip marker and change color, K1, M1; repeat from * at next 3 markers, knit to 1 stitch before button band, M1, K1, change color and K5 (5, 7, 7) sts of button band. (Increase of 10 sts in row.)

Row 8: K5 (5, 7, 7) sts of button band, purl to last 5 (5, 7, 7) sts, changing colors as established, knit button band sts.

Repeat Rows 5–8, 8 (9, 9, 9) more times — 214 (236, 248, 256) sts.

NOTE: You should have 5 (5, 7, 7) sts for button band, for Front 30 (33, 33, 33) sts, sleeve 42 (48, 50, 52) sts, Back 60 (64, 68, 72) sts, sleeve 42 (48, 50, 52) sts, Front 30 (33, 33, 33) sts, and 5 (5, 7, 7) button band.

Sizes 4 and 6 ONLY: Continue to work even with no further increases at the 4 raglan markers as follows:

Next Row: (RS) Knit, changing colors as established.

NOTE: Button bands 5 (5, 7, 7) sts, Fronts 30 (33, 34, 35) sts, sleeves 42 (48, 50, 52) sts, Back 60 (64, 68, 72) sts.

All Sizes: Choose the buttonhole row below for a boy or a girl. Work 2 rows even, changing colors as established, with no further increases — 214 (236, 250, 260) sts.

Buttonhole Row (in right button band for GIRLS): K5 (5, 7, 7), knit to last 5 (5, 7, 7) sts changing colors as established, K2 (2, 3, 3), YO, K2tog, K1 (1, 2, 2).

Buttonhole Row (in left button band for BOYS): K1 (1, 2, 2), K2tog, YO, K2 (2, 3, 3), knit to end of row, changing colors as established.

Next Row: K5 (5, 7, 7), purl to last 5 sts, changing colors as established, K5 (5, 7, 7).

Divide for body and sleeves: (RS) With colors as set, K5 (5, 7, 7), K30 (33, 34, 35) sts for Front, K42 (48, 50, 52) sts for sleeve and then put these 42 (48, 50, 52) sleeve sts onto spare yarn or on a stitch holder; with A K60 (64, 68, 72) sts of Back, K42 (48, 50, 52) sts of sleeve and then put these 42 (48, 50, 52) sleeve sts onto spare yarn or on a stitch holder, K30 (33, 34, 35) sts for Front, K5 (5, 7, 7). Cut yarns B, C, E and the A for the Back only — 130 (140, 150, 156) sts on needle.

body

In the next row change color blocks and cast on underarm stitches to join up the 2 Fronts and the Back:

Next Row: (WS) K5 (5, 7, 7) with A, with C P30 (33, 34, 35) of Front, with C cast on 4 (5, 6, 7) sts at underarm, with E cast on 4 (5, 6, 7) sts, continue with E P30 (32, 34, 36) sts for half of Back, with B P30 (32, 34, 36) sts for second half of Back, with B cast on 4 (5, 6, 7) sts, with D cast on 4 (5, 6, 7) sts, continue with D P30 (33, 34, 35) sts of Front, K5 (5, 7, 7) with A — 146 (160, 174, 184) sts.

Next Row: K5 (5, 7, 7), purl to last 5 (5, 7, 7) sts, changing colors as established, K5 (5, 7, 7) sts.

Next Row (increase at neck edge): K5 (5, 7, 7) in first color, K1, M1, knit, changing colors as established to last 6 (6, 8, 8) sts, M1, K1, change color, K5 (5, 7, 7) — 250 (258) sts.

Next Row: K5 (5, 7, 7), purl to last 5 (5, 7, 7) sts, changing colors as established, K5 (5, 7, 7).

Size 6 ONLY: Repeat last 4 rows above once more — 260 sts.

Work straight changing colors as set. **At the same time** make buttonholes after every 6 (9, 10, 11) ridges on appropriate buttonhole band, until sweater measures 11 (12, 12½, 14½)" from base of collar to needle measuring at Center Back. Leaving A attached, break all other color yarns.

Garter Stitch Bottom Edge
Decrease Row: (RS) With A, K5 (5, 7, 7), K2tog, knit decreasing 8 sts evenly (decrease 2 sts in each of the color sections) to last 7 (7, 9, 9) sts, K2tog, K5 (5, 7, 7) — 136 (150, 164, 174) sts.
Knit 10 (10, 14, 14) rows in Garter Stitch with A.
Bind off.

sleeves: worked in the round
Place sleeve sts on double pointed needles.
Rnd 1: With new color (E for left sleeve, B for right sleeve), and starting at the center underarm, pick up and knit 4 (5, 6, 7) sts from cast on sts at underarm, knit sleeve stitches, pick up and K4 (5, 6, 7) sts from cast on sts, place marker — 50 (58, 62, 66) sts.
Knit 3 rnds.
Decrease Rnd: K1, SSK, knit to last 3 sts, K2tog, K1.
Work Decrease Rnd every following 3rd (3rd, 6th, 6th) rnds 5 (1, 5, 8) more times, then on the following 4th rnd 3 (8, 5, 4) times — 32 (38, 40, 40) sts.
Work even until sleeve measures 5½ (7, 8½, 10½)" from underarm or desired length,
Next Rnd: Knit, decreasing 4 (8, 8, 6) sts evenly across. Cut yarn — 28 (30, 32, 34) sts.

cuff
Rnd 1: With A, knit.
Rnd 2: Purl.
Repeat last 2 rnds 4 (4, 6, 6) more times.
Bind off.

finishing
Weave in ends. Sew on buttons. Sew button band together at Center Back.

dazzling **poncho**

With the current renaissance in ponchos, your young lady will feel up-to-date in this stylish easy-knit model. This little capelet can be worked in contrasting colors, such as red and black for a lady bug effect, or with similar colors like purple with purple trim, embellished with clear beads for a princess effect.

Style Notes: Knit in the round, from the bottom up with no sewing. Add the beads to the garment with the use of a crochet hook as the knitting progresses. Beads come in many sizes and shapes. Make sure that the hole in the barrel is large enough to accommodate the crochet hook and the yarn. If beads are unavailable, substitute a purl stitch for the bead and sew on colorful buttons over the purl stitches instead!

Designer: Dana Gibbons
Experience Level: Intermediate

sizes
To fit Child: 2–4 (6–8) years

finished measurements
Chest: 34 (40)" around middle of capelet
Length: 16 (19)" from base of hood to bottom edge
Bottom width: 56 (76)" around bottom

materials
Chunky Weight Yarn (3.5 ounces/110 yards,
   100 grams/101 meters per ball):
      Red or Purple (MC) 4 (5) balls
DK, Light Worsted Weight Yarn (eyelash novelty)
   (1.75 ounces/96 yards, 50 grams/90 meters
   per ball):
      Black or Purple (trim) 2 (3) balls
Size 10 (6.0 mm) 24" (60 cm) circular needle

Set of size 10 (6.0 mm) double pointed needles for 3-Needle Bind Off

Size D (3.0 mm) crochet hook or size to fit through hole in pony beads

Darning needle

48 (52) pony beads

4 markers in different colors

Stitch holder or large safety pin

gauge

15 sts = 4" (10 cm) on size 10 (6.0 mm) needle in Stockinette Stitch or size needed to obtain gauge

abbreviations

B1 (bead 1): Insert crochet hook into a bead then into the next stitch knitwise (as if you were going to knit the stitch). Slip stitch onto crochet hook and pull the stitch through the bead. Slip stitch back onto left needle by inserting the left needle into the stitch on the hook with the point going towards the hook (prevents a twisted stitch). The stitch is back on left needle with bead below the needle. Knit the stitch as usual. Bead drops to previous rnd.

beginning at the bottom

With size 10 (6.0 mm) circular needle and 2 strands of eyelash yarn held together as you work, loosely cast on 200 (218) sts. Place "beginning of rnd" marker and join in the rnd, being careful not to twist stitches. **NOTE:** Make the "beginning of rnd" marker different in some way by using a different color or tie a bright piece of yarn to the marker. This way you will always know where to begin.

Rnd 1: Slip "beginning of rnd" marker, P100 (109) sts, place second marker, purl to end of the rnd.

(Markers are placed at Center Front and Center Back of poncho.)

Knit 1 rnd.

Purl 1 rnd.

Repeat last 2 rnds twice more. Cut eyelash yarn. (4 Garter Stitch ridges made.)

Change to MC.

Using a single strand of MC, knit 2 (3) rnds.

decreasing

Decrease Rnd: *Slip marker, K1, SSK, knit to 3 sts before the next marker, K2tog, K1; repeat from * once more to end of rnd — 196 (214) sts.

Knit 1 (2) rnd(s).

Repeat last 2 (3) rnds twice more — 188 (206) sts.

Work Decrease Rnd once more — 184 (202) sts.

Bead Rnd: *Slip marker, K5, B1, work [K8, B1] to last 5 sts before marker, K5; repeat from * once more.

Decrease Rnd: *Slip marker, K1, SSK, knit to last 3 sts before marker, K2tog, K1; repeat from * once more — 180 (198) sts.

Knit 1 rnd.

Repeat last 2 rnds 8 more times — 148 (166) sts.

Work Decrease Rnd once more — 144 (162) sts.

Bead Rnd: This set of beads should line up directly above the first set. *Slip marker, K4, B1, work [K8, B1] to 4 sts before marker, K4; repeat from * once more.

Work Decrease Rnd.

Knit 1 rnd.

Repeat last 2 rnds 7 more times —112 (130) sts.

Shoulder shaping: It would be helpful at this point to use different colors for the two shoulder markers than the two center markers. Decreases at the shoulder are worked every other rnd; decreases at the Center Front and Back are worked in next and every following 4th rnd.

Rnd 1: Slip "beginning of rnd" marker, K1, SSK, K22 (27), K2tog, K1, place shoulder marker, K1, SSK, K22 (26), K2tog, K1, slip Center Back marker, K1, SSK, K22 (26), K2tog, K1, place shoulder marker, K1, SSK, K22 (27), K2tog, K1 — 104 (122) sts.

NOTE: You now have 4 markers in place: "beginning of rnd" marker at the Center Front, one at the right shoulder, one at the Center Back, and one at the left shoulder which is the same color as the right shoulder marker. Keeping the Center Front and Back markers in one color and the 2 shoulder markers in a second color makes it much easier to identify where to place the decreases.

Rnd 2: Knit.

Rnd 3 (decrease at shoulder markers only): Knit to 3 sts before shoulder marker, K2tog, K1, slip shoulder marker, K1, SSK, knit around to 3 sts before next shoulder marker, K2tog, K1, slip shoulder marker, K1, SSK, knit to end of rnd. Do not decrease at the two center markers — 100 (118) sts.

Bead Rnd: Slip marker, K4, B1, [K8, B1] twice, K2 (7), slip marker, K2 (7), B1, [K8, B1] twice, K4 (3), slip marker, K4 (3), B1, [K8, B1] 2 times, K2 (7), slip marker, K2 (7), B1, [K8, B1] 2 times, K4.

Rnd 5 (decrease at all 4 markers): *K1, SSK, knit to

3 sts before next marker, K2tog, K1, slip marker; repeat from * 3 times (8 sts decreased) — 92, (110) sts.

Rnd 6: Knit.

Rnd 7 (decrease at 2 shoulder markers only): Knit to 3 sts before shoulder marker, K2tog, K1, slip shoulder marker, K1, SSK, knit around to 3 sts before next shoulder marker, K2tog, K1, slip shoulder marker, K1, SSK, knit to end of rnd — 88 (106) sts.

Rnd 8: Knit.
Repeat Rnds 5–8 once more — 76 (94) sts.

Begin Short Row Shaping for Hood

To shape for the hood, work extra rows across the Back of the poncho. These are called short rows because you will knit only partway around only and turn (leaving sts on the needle unworked), then you will purl back across the WS as follows:

Short Row 1 (decrease at 3 markers): (RS) Beginning at the Center Front, knit to 3 sts before shoulder marker, K2tog, K1, slip shoulder marker, K1, SSK, knit to 3 sts before the Center Back marker, K2tog, K1, slip Back marker, K1, SSK, knit to 3 sts before the second shoulder marker, K2tog, K1, slip shoulder marker, K1, SSK, knit to 4 sts before end of rnd, TURN (leaving 4 sts unworked) — 70 (88) sts on needle, including the unworked sts.

Short Row 2: With WS of poncho facing, SL1(p), purl to 4 sts before end of rnd; TURN, leaving these sts unworked.

Short Row 3 (decrease at 2 shoulder markers only): (RS) SL1(k), knit, decreasing as set at shoulder markers only, knit to 8 sts before end of rnd; TURN — 66 (84) sts, including the unworked sts.

Short Row 4: (WS) SL1(p), purl to 8 sts before end of rnd; TURN.

Short Row 5 (decrease at 3 markers): SL1(k), knit, decreasing at all 3 markers as set to 12 sts before end of rnd; TURN — 60 (78) sts, including the unworked sts.

Short Row 6: (WS) SL1(p), purl to 12 sts before end of rnd; TURN.

Short Row 7 (decrease at 2 shoulder markers only): SL1(k), knit, decreasing at shoulder markers only, to last 4 sts of rnd, knitting 8 of the unworked sts on hold — 56 (74) sts, including the unworked sts.

Short Row 8: (WS) SL1(p), purl to last 4 sts, removing shoulder and Center Back markers, purling 8 of the unworked sts on hold.

hood

Work back and forth on circular needle for hood. Put 4 sts on either side of the Center Front marker, including the marker, on a stitch holder or large safety pin (8 sts on holder) — 48 (66) sts on needle.

For Large Size ONLY:
Decrease Row: *K2, K2tog; repeat from * to last 2 sts, K2 — 50 sts.
Purl 1 row.

For BOTH SIZES: (48, 50 sts)
Knit 1 row.
Purl 1 row.
Repeat last 2 rows for total of 10 (11)" from beginning of hood. Place half of stitches on a size 10 (6.0 mm) double pointed needle. Turn hood inside out and bind off using 3-Needle Bind Off method with RS of hood facing. (Optional: Bind off all sts while still on circular needle. Sew hood seam.)

Hood Trim (in Garter Stitch)

Pick Up Rnd: Place the 8 sts on holder onto the circular needle and using 2 strands of eyelash yarn held together and circular needle, pick up and knit 1 stitch at bottom of hood edge, place marker, pick up and knit 2 sts for every 3 rows around hood opening, placing another marker before last stitch picked up, TURN (do not knit 8 sts on hold).

Row 1: (WS) SL1(p), slip marker, knit to next marker, slip marker, P2tog, (1 stitch from hood edge and 1 stitch from Front sts on hold); TURN.

Row 2: SL1(k), slip marker, knit to next marker, slip marker, K2tog, (1 stitch from hood edge and 1 stitch from Front sts on hold); TURN.

Repeat last 2 rows until all of the sts have been worked off the Front sts on hold; TURN.

Next Row: SL1(p), knit to end of rnd, removing all markers as you go.
Bind off loosely, leaving a 4" tail at end. Cut yarn.

finishing

Weave in all ends.

dazzling
beaded bag

This little beaded bag, a fun and easy project, is a perfect accessory to the poncho. On its own it gives the illusion of a ladybug when done in red and black.

Style Notes: See page 18.
Designer: Dana Gibbons
Experience Level: Intermediate
One size

materials

Chunky Weight Yarn (3.5 ounces/110 yards, 100 grams/101 meters per ball):
> Purple or Red (MC) 1 ball

DK, Light Worsted Weight Yarn (eyelash novelty) (1.75 ounces/96 yards, 50 grams/ 90 meters per ball):
> Purple or Black (trim) 1 ball

Size 10 (6.0 mm) 16" (40 cm) circular needle
Size 3 (3.0 mm) crochet hook or size to fit through hole in pony beads
14 pony beads
2 ¾-inch shank buttons
2 small shirt buttons
2 markers, different colors if possible

gauge

14 sts = 4" (10 cm) with MC yarn on size 10 (6.0 mm) needles or size needed to obtain gauge

B1 (bead 1): Insert crochet hook into a bead then into the next stitch knitwise (as if you were going to knit the stitch). Slip stitch onto crochet hook and pull the stitch through the bead. Slip stitch back onto left needle by inserting the left needle into the stitch on

the hook with the point going towards the hook (prevents a twisted stitch). The stitch is back on left needle with bead below the needle. Knit the stitch as usual. Bead drops to previous rnd.

flap

With circular needle and eyelash yarn, holding two strands of eyelash together as you work, cast on 8 sts.

Work back and forth with circular needle:
Row 1: Knit.
Row 2: K1, Kfb in next st, K4, Kfb in next st, K1 — 10 sts.
Row 3: Knit.
Row 4: K1, Kfb next st, K6, Kfb next st, K1 — 12 sts.
Row 5: Knit.
Row 6: K1, Kfb in next st, knit to last 2 sts, Kfb in next st, K1
Row 7: Knit.
Repeat Rows 6 and 7 until 20 sts on needle.
Knit 2 more rows.

Buttonholes: K5, K2tog, YO, K6, YO, K2tog, K5.
Knit 7 rows. Cut eyelash yarn, leaving tail.

top edging

Attach MC.
NOTE: Do not weave in the tails of the colors at this point, as they will show. It is better to weave in the ends when project is complete.
Knit 2 rows with MC
Next Row: Knit to end of row, cast on 22 sts — 42 sts.

Join in the rnd, being careful not to twist sts; place marker for beginning of rnd.

Working in the rnd:
Rnd 1: Purl 20 sts, place second marker, P22.
Rnd 2: K20, slip marker, SL1, K20, SL1.
Rnd 3: P20, slip marker, K1, P20, K1.

body

Rnd 1: K20, slip marker, SL1, K20, SL1.
Rnd 2: Knit.
Repeat Rnds 1 and 2, twice more.
First Bead Rnd: K6, B1, K6, B1, K6, slip marker, SL1, K6, B1, K6, B1, K6, SL1.

Next Rnd: Knit.

Repeat Rnds 1 and 2, 4 times — 8 rnds total.

Second Bead Rnd: K3, B1, K5, B1, K6, B1, K3, slip marker, SL1, K3, B1, K6, B1, K5, B1, K3, SL1.

Next Rnd: Knit.

Repeat Rnds 1 and 2, 4 times.

Repeat first bead rnd once more.

Next Rnd: Knit.

Repeat Rnds 1 and 2 once more.

bottom

Next Rnd: P20, slip marker, with yarn in back SL1, P20, with yarn in back SL1.

Next Rnd: Knit.

Next Rnd: P20, slip marker, with yarn in back SL1, P20, with yarn in back SL1.

Next Rnd: Slip 21 sts to a spare double pointed needle (size does not matter). Remove markers as you go. With WS together, working on the RS, work 3-Needle Bind Off.

Weave in any ends, taking yarns into the inside of the purse.

finishing

Twisted Purse Handle: Cut one strand of each yarn 60 inches long. Knot together at each end. Have someone hold one end, or place on a small hook. (I remove a picture from the wall and use the small hanging hook). Twist the yarns, holding the knot at all times. Yarns will twist around each other. When yarns seem quite tight, bring the two knots together, and tie into one knot. The yarns will fold in half and twist together, approximately 21–23 inches long. Gently pull

at the cord to smooth. Tie each end just above the slip stitches in the purse. Cut off any excess length.

Sew buttons on the top edging of the second set of cast on stitches, lining them up with the button-holes. After two to three passes of the thread, attach the small shirt button to the WS and sew through both buttons. This adds stability and strength to the button attachment.

autumn **stripes**

Here is a simple, classic top down pullover suitable for boys or girls. If you have never knit from the top down, this is an excellent first time project. This sweater starts with a mock turtleneck collar. Work increases every other round at the four raglan shapelines to the underarms. The sleeve stitches are put on spare yarn and the body is knit in the round to the desired length. The sleeves are then knit as long as required.

The beauty of knitting for children from the top down is that you can adjust the sleeve and body lengths as you knit along and easily add to them as the child grows or the sweater is passed down in the family.

You can knit the stripes in this sweater in a variety of ways. Instead of using two colors, you could knit four rounds in the main color using three different contrast colors, one after the other, down the sweater. You could also knit the sweater in large blocks of color for the ultimate in simplicity.

This raglan sweater does not have a designated front or back, so it cannot be put on backwards by the little person for whom you are knitting.

Style Notes: Knit from the top down with no sewing required.

Designer: Lynda Gemmell
Experience Level: Beginner

sizes
To fit Child: 1 (2, 4, 6) years

finished measurements
Chest: 24 (26, 28½, 30½)"
Body Length: 12 (13½, 14½, 17)"
Sleeve Length: 6 (7½, 9½, 12)"

materials
Chunky Weight Yarn (3.5 ounces/110 yards,
   100 grams/101 meters per ball):
      Blue or Orange (MC) 2 (2, 3, 3) balls
      Light Blue or Gold (CC) 2 (2, 2, 3) balls
Size 10 (6.0 mm) 16" (40 cm) circular needle
Set of size 10 (6.0 mm) double pointed needles
Optional for sizes 4 and 6 only:
Size 10 (6.0 mm) 24" (60 cm) circular needle
4 markers

gauge
14 sts = 4" (10 cm) on size 10 (6.0 mm) needle or size needed to obtain gauge

begin with the mock turtleneck
With size 10 (6.0 mm) circular needle and MC, cast on 63 (63, 64, 64) sts. Place marker for beginning of rnd and join in the rnd, being careful not to twist.
Sizes 1 and 2 ONLY: Decrease Rnd: *K2, P2tog, P1, K2, P2; repeat from * to end of rnd — 56 sts.
All Sizes:
Rib Rnd: *K2, P2; repeat from * to end of rnd — 56 (56, 64, 64) sts.
Repeat Rib Rnd until the collar measures 1 (1½, 1½, 2)" from cast on edge.
Next Rnd: Knit.

yoke
The yoke of the sweater starts with a CC stripe and the placement of markers for the shapelines of the raglan shoulder shaping. Each shapeline consists of 2 stitches separating the pair of increases and creates the distinctive diagonal line of the raglan yoke. Place a marker before each of these 2-stitch shapelines. On

every other rnd, you will be increasing 1 stitch before the 2-stitch shapeline and increasing 1 stitch after to make 4 raglan lines for the yoke.

Marker Rnd: With CC, slip "beginning of rnd" marker, K2 (shapeline), K18 (18, 22, 22) for body. Place marker, K2 (shapeline), K6 for sleeve. Place marker, K2 (shapeline), K18 (18, 22, 22) for body. Place marker, K2 (shapeline), K6 for sleeve — 56 (56, 64, 64) sts.
NOTE: Put something special on the first marker to indicate the "beginning of the rnd" or use a different colored marker.

NOTE: Each Increase Rnd starts with a M1 Increase **before** the first shapeline marker (with "beginning of rnd" marker still on left needle, work the first M1 increase and then slip "beginning of rnd" marker over to right needle and continue), so that this increase is not forgotten at the end of the rnd.
Increase Rnd: With CC, M1, slip "beginning of rnd" marker, K2, M1, K18 (18, 22, 22) sts, M1, slip marker, K2, M1, K6, M1, slip marker, K2, M1, K18 (18, 22, 22) sts, M1, slip marker, K2, M1, knit to end of rnd — 64 (64, 72, 72) sts on needle.
NOTE: You should now have 8 more stitches on your needle for a total of 64 (64, 72, 72) sts. Each successive Increase Rnd will add 8 more stitches.

pattern stripes

Next Rnd: With MC, knit.
Increase Rnd: With MC, *M1, slip marker, K2, M1, knit to next marker; repeat from * 3 more times.
Repeat last 2 rnds once more.

Next Rnd: With CC, knit.
Increase Rnd: With CC, *M1, slip marker, K2, M1, knit to next marker; repeat from * 3 more times.

NOTE: Carry the 2 colors up the inside of the sweater loosely so as not to pull the fabric.

Repeat the Pattern Stripes sequence of 6 rnds above, until there are 128 (144, 152, 168) sts on the needle.

NOTE: The Front and Back should both have 38 (42, 46, 50) sts between the markers, and each sleeve should have 26 (30, 30, 34) sts between the markers.

Continue to knit every rnd, maintaining the stripes as set, without any more increases, until the yoke measures 5½ (6, 6½, 7)" from the first CC rnd to needle. The yoke can be lengthened if you wish by continuing to knit extra rnds even — 128 (144, 152, 168) sts.

divide for the sleeves and body
NOTE: The 2 shapeline stitches belong to the body and stay on the circular needle.
Next Rnd: Slip "beginning of rnd" marker, *K38 (42, 46, 50), remove marker, K2, knit next 24 (28, 28, 32) sleeve sts and put these 24 (28, 28, 32) sleeve sts onto a spare piece of yarn; repeat from * once more — 80 (88, 96, 104) sts on circular needle.

body
Next Rnd: Slip "beginning of rnd" marker, K40 (44, 48, 52), cast on 2 sts, K40 (44, 48, 52) sts, cast on 2 sts — 84 (92, 100, 108) sts.
Knit every rnd, continuing with the stripes as set, until the sweater measures 11 (12, 13, 15)" or desired length, measuring from the first CC stripe below the neckband. End with a completed stripe. Note: For the larger sizes, you may wish to knit with a longer circular needle 24" (60 cm).
The next color stripe forms the bottom edge.

NOTE: I ended after finishing a CC stripe so bottom ribbing is in MC but you can also end after a MC stripe and do the ribbing in the CC.

bottom edge

Decrease Rnd: With next color of stripe pattern, *K8 (2, 4, 6), K2tog, [K6, K2tog] 3 (5, 5, 5) times, K8 (2, 4, 6); repeat from * once more — 76 (80, 88, 96) sts.
Rib Rnd: Continue with same color, *K2, P2; repeat from * to end of rnd.
Repeat Rib Rnd for 1 (1½, 1½, 2)".
Bind off in rib.

sleeve

With double pointed needles and appropriate color to maintain stripe pattern as set, starting at the center of the cast on underarm sts, pick up, and knit 1 stitch; knit all the sleeve stitches from the spare yarn, pick up and knit the remaining 1 stitch from the underarm — 26 (30, 30, 34) sts.
NOTE: Leave an 8" tail when joining in the yarn to tidy up the underarm later.

Knit every rnd, changing colors for the stripes as you go, until the sleeve measures 5 (6, 8, 10)" from underarm or knit the sleeves as long as the child you are knitting for requires. End with a completed stripe. The next color forms the cuff.

cuff

Decrease Rnd: With next color in stripe pattern, *K2tog, K11 (13, 13, 15); repeat from * to end of rnd — 24 (28, 28, 32) sts.
Rib Rnd: Continue with same color, *K2, P2; repeat from * to end of rnd.
Repeat Rib Rnd for 1 (1½, 1½, 2)".
Bind off.
NOTE: As the child grows, you can always add to the sleeves by ripping back the cuff and knitting another stripe or two.

finishing

Sew in ends. Use the long tails at underarm to tidy up any underarm holes.

princess cables
tunic and hat

Curiosity played a roll in this all over cable design. Could the simplicity of a top down, no sew sweater be teamed with an easy cable to create an aran look for a little princess? The answer was, YES!

Style Notes: Knit from the top down. No sewing. Easy twisted cable pattern.

Designer: Mary K Hobbs
Experience Level: Advanced

sizes

To fit Child: 2 (4, 6) years
Chest Size: 22 (24, 26)"

finished measurements

Sweater:

Chest: 26 (28, 30)"
Body Length: 13 (15, 17)"
Sleeve Length: 8 (10, 12)"
Hat:
Head Circumference: 17 (18, 19)"

materials

DK, Light Worsted Weight Yarn (3.5 ounces/
    250 yards, 100 grams/230 meters per ball):
        Pink or Yellow Tunic: 3 (3, 4) balls
        Pink or Yellow Hat: 1 ball
Size 8 (5.0 mm) 16" (40 cm) circular needle
Size 6 (4.0 mm) 16" (40 cm) circular needle
Size 6 (4.0 mm) 24" (60 cm) circular needle
Set of size 6 (4.0 mm) double pointed needles
    for the hat and sleeves
4 markers

gauge

22 stitches = 4" (10 cm) on size 6 (4.0 mm) needle in Stockinette Stitch or size needed to obtain gauge

Twist 2: K2tog but do not slip off needle, then insert right-hand needle between these 2 stitches and knit the first stitch again, slipping both stitches off needle together.

Twisted Cable Rib Pattern:
Rnd 1: *K2, P2; repeat from * to end of rnd.
Rnds 2 and 3: Repeat Rnd 1.
Rnd 4: *Twist 2, P2; repeat from * to end of rnd.
Twist 2: K2tog but do not slip off needles, then insert right-hand needle between these 2 stitches and knit the first stitch again, slipping both stitches off needle together.

tunic

Begin at the Collar

With size 8 (5.0 mm) needle, cast on 80 (88, 96) sts. Using the size 6 (4.0 mm) needle, knit 1 rnd. Join in the rnd, taking care not to twist stitches. Place a marker to indicate the beginning of the rnd.
Knit 5 more rnds.

Work in Twisted Cable Rib Pattern as follows:
Rnd 1: *K2, P2; repeat from * to end of rnd.
Rnds 2 and 3: Repeat Rnd 1.
Rnd 4: *Twist 2, P2; repeat from * to end of rnd.
Repeat Rnds 1 and 2 once more.

yoke

Use four shapelines to increase on the yoke. Each shapeline consists of 2 stitches (a cable) that creates the distinctive diagonal lines for the raglan yoke. Increases are worked on every other rnd before and after each of the shapeline cables. In the next rnd, you will place a marker before each shapeline cable. **NOTE:** Make the first marker different in some way (a different color marker or tie a piece of colored yarn to it) so that you will know where each rnd begins.

Marker Rnd: Slip "beginning of rnd" marker, *K2 (shapeline sts), work 30 (30, 34) sts in pattern as established (for body), place marker, K2 (shapeline sts), work next 6 (10, 10) sts in pattern as established (for sleeve), place marker*; repeat from * to * once more, ending at beginning marker.

NOTE: Increases are indicated by "M1(p)" or "M1(k)". No holes are created when using M1 increases and they are made purlwise or knitwise in order to work the increased stitches into pattern as soon as possible. Two purled stitches will always be on either side of the cable shapelines.

Increase Rnd: *Slip marker, Twist 2 (shapeline cable), P2, M1(p), Twist 2, [P2, Twist 2] 6 (6, 7) times, M1(p), P2, slip marker, Twist 2 (shapeline cable), P2, M1(p), Twist 2, [P2, Twist 2] 0 (1, 1) time, M1(p), P2; repeat from * once more — 88 (96, 104) sts.

Next Rnd: *Slip marker, K2 (shapeline cable), P3, K2, [P2, K2] 6 (6, 7) times, P3, slip marker, K2 (shapeline cable), P3, K2, [P2, k2] 0 (1, 1) time, P3; repeat from * once more.

Next Increase Rnd: *Slip marker, K2 (shapeline cable), P2, M1(p), P1, K2, [P2, K2] 6 (6, 7) times, P1, M1(p), P2, slip marker, K2 (shapeline cable), P2, M1(p), P1, K2, [P2, K2] 0 (1, 1) time, P1, M1(p), P2; repeat from * once more — 96 (104, 112) sts.

Next Rnd: *Slip marker, K2 (shapeline cable), P4, K2, [P2, K2] 6 (6, 7) times, P4, slip marker, K2 (shapeline cable), P4, K2, [P2, K2] 0 (1, 1) time, P4; repeat from * once more.

Next Increase Rnd: *Slip marker, Twist 2 (shapeline cable), P2, M1(k), [P2, Twist 2] 7 (7, 8) times, P2, M1(k), P2, slip marker, Twist 2 (shapeline cable), P2, M1(k), [P2, Twist 2] 1 (2, 2) times, P2, M1(k), P2; repeat from * once more — 104 (112, 120) sts.

Next Rnd: *Slip marker, K2 (shapeline cable), P2, K1, [P2, K2] 7 (7, 8) times, P2, K1, P2, slip marker, K2 (shapeline cable), P2, K1, [P2, K2] 1 (2, 2) times, P2, K1, P2; repeat from * once more.

Next Increase Rnd: *Slip marker, K2 (shapeline cable), P2, M1(k), K1, [P2, K2] 7 (7, 8) times, P2, K1, M1(k), P2, slip marker, K2 (shapeline cable), P2, M1(k), K1, [P2, K2] 1 (2, 2) times, P2, K1, M1(k), P2; repeat from * once more — 112 (120, 128) sts.

Next Rnd: *Slip marker, K2 (shapeline cable), [P2, K2] 9 (9, 10) times, P2, slip marker, K2 (shapeline cable), [P2, K2] 3 (4, 4) times, P2; repeat from * once more.

Continue increasing in this manner until there are 296 (312, 328) sts on your needle. End after working a "Twist 2" rnd. Note: Change to longer size 6 (4.0 mm) 24" (60 cm) circular needle when the increased number of stitches becomes too many for the shorter needle. There should be 62 (66, 70) sts between the shapeline cables for each sleeve and 86 (90, 94) sts, including the shapeline cable sts, for both the body sections.

NOTE: Since this is a cable rib, the rib will draw the fabric in, so it will seem to be narrow, but when the piece is completed, it will be blocked to size. Therefore, when measuring the piece vertically, be sure to stretch out the ribbed fabric a bit horizontally. That way when the piece is blocked to size, it will be the desired length.

If the yoke is not yet 7 (7½, 8)" deep, measuring vertically from the center base of the collar down to your needle, continue to work in pattern, with no further increases until you have reached the length above. End after working a "Twist 2" rnd.

Divide body and sleeves: The Divide Rnd below will separate the sleeves and the body. The sleeve stitches will now be held on spare yarn as you work the body first. The body stitches stay on the circular needle and stitches are cast on at the underarms. The shapeline cables will be included with the body stitches.

Divide Rnd: Removing markers as you go, *work in pattern to next marker, then work next 2 sts (you should have 86 [90, 94] body sts, which stay on the circular needle). Work in pattern to next marker and

thread these 62 (66, 70) sts onto a spare piece of yarn for the sleeve; repeat from * once more — 172 (180, 188) sts on needle for the body.

body

Next Rnd: Place a marker for the beginning of the rnd, *work in pattern to underarm, cast on 6 sts; repeat from * once more — 184 (192, 200) sts.
Continue every rnd in pattern, until the sweater measures 13 (15, 17)" from the base of the collar down to the needle or the desired length. End after working a "Twist 2" rnd. Bind off ribwise.

sleeves

With RS facing, look at the underarm. There are 6 sts (the cast on sts on body) and since these have been worked in pattern, the center 2 sts are a cable. This cable will now be a seamline for the underarm. A couple of decreases will be made to bring the sleeves into pattern.

Set-up Rnd: Using double pointed needles, with RS facing, start with the underarm cable, pick up and knit these center 2 sts, pick up and purl the next 2 sts, now work sleeve stitches off spare yarn in pattern around sleeve, pick up and purl last 2 underarm sts — 68 (72, 76) sts.

Next Rnd: K2 (cable sts), P4, work remaining sleeve sts in pattern, ending with P4.
Next Rnd: As the last rnd.
Decrease Rnd: Twist 2, P2tog, P2, continue around sleeve in pattern to last 2 sts, P2tog — 66 (70, 74) sts. Work three more rnds in pattern, noting that there will be 3 purled sts on either side of the underarm cable.

Next Decrease Rnd: Twist 2, P2tog, P1, continue around sleeve in pattern to last 2 sts, P2tog — 64 (68, 72) sts.

NOTE: Due to the nature of the ribbed pattern, it is not necessary to make further decreases to taper the sleeves.

Work in pattern, with no further decreases, until sleeve measures 7½ (9½, 11½)" from underarm or ½" shy of desired length for the recipient of the sweater. End after working a "Twist 2" rnd.

cuff

Next Rnd: *K2, P2tog; repeat from * to end of rnd — 48 (51, 54) sts.
Next Rnd: Knit, decreasing 8 (7, 10) sts evenly around — 40 (44, 44) sts.
Knit 5 more rnds.
Bind off.

finishing

Sew in ends so that they cannot be seen when the cuffs roll up.

hat

Using size 6 (4.0 mm) double pointed needles, cast on 56 (60, 64) sts.
Join in the rnd, taking care not to twist stitches.
Place a marker to indicate the beginning of the rnd.
Work 6 rnds in Stockinette Stitch (knit every rnd).
Next Rnd: *K1, P1; repeat from * to end of rnd.
Repeat the last rnd once more.
Eyelet Rnd: *P2tog, YRN; repeat from * to end of rnd. (Eyelet holes will allow for the threading of an I-cord to draw the top of the hat closed.)

Next Rnd: *K1, P1; repeat from * to end of rnd.
Repeat the last rnd once more.
Increase Rnd: *K1, M1(k), P1, M1(p); repeat from * to end of rnd, doubling the number of stitches — 112 (120, 128) sts.

Change to the size 6 (4.0 mm) 16" (40 cm) circular needle or continue using the double pointed needles, whichever you prefer.

Work Twisted Cable Rib Pattern as follows:
Rnd 1: *K2, P2; repeat from * to end of rnd.
Rnds 2 and 3: Repeat Rnd 1.
Rnd 4: *Twist 2, P2; repeat from * to end of rnd.
Repeat these last 4 rnds until hat measures 4½ (5, 5½)" from just below Eyelet Rnd. End after a "Twist 2" rnd.

Decrease Rnd: *K2tog, K6; repeat from * to end of rnd — 98 (105, 112) sts.
Knit 5 rnds. These last knit rnds will roll to form a brim.
Bind off.
Sew in the ends. The end of the bind off rnd should be sewn in on the RS, so that when the brim rolls, it will not show.

I-Cord

Using size 6 (4.0 mm) double pointed needles, cast on 3 sts and knit a 16" I-cord. Sew in ends. (See page 5 for I-cord instructions.) Weave the I-cord in and out of the eyelet holes at the top of the hat. Draw up to desired tightness. (Note: If your little recipient has a ponytail, the ponytail could be drawn up through the hole.) Knot each end of the I-cord.

twisted cables
pullover and hat

This design is perfect for the little princess or prince in your life. The simplicity of a top down, no sew pullover with a yoke of cables and cabled cuffs complete this look.

Style Notes: Knit from the top down with no sewing. Easy twisted cable stitch.

Designer: Mary K Hobbs
Experience Level: Intermediate

sizes
To fit Child: 2 (4, 6) years
Chest Size: 22 (24, 26)"

finished measurements
Sweater:
Chest: 26 (28, 30)"
Body Length: 13 (15, 17)"
Sleeve Length: 8 (10, 12)"
Hat:
Head Circumference: 17 (18, 19)"

materials
DK, Light Worsted Weight Yarn (1.75 ounces /
    129 yards, 50 grams/119 meters per ball):
        Blue or Beige Hat 1 (1, 2) balls
        Blue or Beige Pullover 4 (5, 6) balls
Size 8 (5.0 mm) 16" (40 cm) circular needle
Size 6 (4.0 mm) 16" (40 cm) circular needle
Size 6 (4.0 mm) 24" (60 cm) circular needle
Set of size 6 (4.0 mm) double pointed needles
    for the hat and sleeves
4 markers

gauge

22 stitches = 4" (10 cm) size 6 (4.0 mm) needle in Stockinette Stitch or needle needed to obtain gauge

Twist 2: K2tog but do not slip off needle, then insert right-hand needle between these 2 stitches and knit the first stitch again, slipping both stitches off needle together.

Twisted Cable Rib Pattern:

Rnd 1: *K2, P2; rep from * to end of rnd.

Rnds 2 and 3: Repeat Rnd 1.

Rnd 4: *Twist 2, P2; repeat from * to end of rnd.

pullover

Begin at the Collar

With size 8 (5.0 mm) needles, cast on 80 (88, 96) sts. Join in the rnd, taking care not to twist your stitches. Using the size 6 (4.0 mm) 16" (40 cm) needle, work in Twisted Cable Rib Pattern as follows:

Rnd 1: Place a marker to indicate the beginning of the rnd, *K2, P2; repeat from * to end of rnd.

Rnds 2 and 3: *K2, P2; repeat from * to end of rnd.

Rnd 4: *Twist 2, P2; repeat from * to end of rnd. Repeat Rnds 1 and 2 once more.

yoke

Use four shapelines to increase on the yoke. Each shapeline consists of 2 stitches (a cable) that creates the distinctive diagonal lines for the raglan yoke. Work increases on every other rnd before and after each of the shapeline cables. In the next rnd, you will place a marker before each shapeline cable.

NOTE: Make the first marker different in some way (a different color or tie a piece of colored yarn to it) so that you will know where each rnd begins.

Marker Rnd: Slip "beginning of rnd" marker, *K2 (shapeline sts), work 30 (30, 34) sts in pattern as established for body, place marker, K2 (shapeline sts), work next 6 (10, 10) sts in pattern as established for sleeve*, place marker; repeat from * to * once more, ending at beginning marker.

NOTE: Increases are indicated by "M1(p)" or "M1(k)". No holes are created when using M1 increases and they are made purlwise or knitwise in order to work the increased stitches into pattern as soon as possible. Two purled stitches will always be on either side of the cable shapelines.

Next Rnd (Increase Rnd): *Slip marker, Twist 2 (shapeline cable), P2, M1(p), Twist 2, [P2, Twist 2] 6 (6, 7) times, M1(p), P2, slip marker, Twist 2 (shapeline cable), P2, M1(p), Twist 2, [P2, Twist 2] 0 (1, 1) time, M1(p), P2; repeat from * once more — 88 (96, 104) sts.

Next Rnd: *Slip marker, K2 (shapeline cable), P3, K2, [P2, K2] 6 (6, 7) times, P3, slip marker, K2 (shapeline cable), P3, K2, [P2, k2] 0 (1, 1) time, P3; repeat from * once more.

Next Rnd (Increase Rnd): *Slip marker, K2 (shapeline cable), P2, M1(p), P1, K2, [P2, K2] 6 (6, 7) times, P1, M1(p), P2, slip marker, K2 (shapeline cable), P2, M1(p), P1, K2, [P2, k2] 0 (1,1) time, P1, M1(p), P2; repeat from * once more — 96 (104, 112) sts.

Next Rnd: *Slip marker, K2 (shapeline cable), P4, K2, [P2, K2] 6 (6, 7) times, P4, slip marker, K2 (shapeline cable), P4, K2, [P2, K2] 0 (1, 1) time, P4; repeat from * once more.

Next Rnd (Increase Rnd): *Slip marker, Twist 2 (shapeline cable), P2, M1(k), [P2, Twist 2] 7 (7, 8) times, P2, M1(k), P2, slip marker, Twist 2 (shapeline cable), P2, M1(k), [P2, Twist 2] 1 (2, 2) times, P2, M1(k), P2; rep from * once more — 104 (112, 120) sts.

Next Rnd: *Slip marker, K2 (shapeline cable), P2, K1, [P2, K2] 7 (7, 8) times, P2, K1, P2, slip marker, K2 (shapeline cable), P2, K1, [P2, K2] 1 (2, 2) times, P2, K1, P2; repeat from * once more.

Next Rnd (Increase Rnd): *Slip marker, K2 (shapeline cable), P2, M1(k), K1, [P2, K2] 7 (7, 8) times, P2, K1, M1(k), P2, slip marker, K2 (shapeline cable), P2, M1(k), K1, [P2, K2] 1 (2, 2) times, P2, K1, M1(k), P2; rep from * once more — 112 (120, 128) sts.

Next Rnd: *Slip marker, K2 (shapeline cable), [P2, K2] 9 (9, 10) times, P2, slip marker, K2 (shapeline cable), [P2, K2] 3 (4, 4) times, P2; repeat from * once more.

Continue increasing in this manner until there are 296 (312, 328) sts on your needle. End after working a "Twist 2" rnd. Change to a longer size 6 (4.0 mm) 24" (60 cm) circular needle when the increased number of sts becomes too many for the shorter needle. There should be 62 (66, 70) sts between the shapeline cables for each sleeve and 86 (90, 94) sts, (including the shapeline cable sts), for both of the body sections.

NOTE: Since this is a cable rib, the rib will draw the fabric in, so it will seem to be narrow, but when the piece is completed, it will be blocked to size. Therefore, when measuring the piece vertically, be sure to stretch out the ribbed fabric a bit horizontally. That way when the piece is blocked to size, it will be the desired length.
If the yoke is not yet 7 (7½, 8)" deep, measuring vertically from the center base of the collar down to your needle, continue to work in pattern, with no further increases until you have reached the length above. End after working a "Twist 2" rnd.

Divide Body and Sleeves: The Divide Rnd below will separate the sleeves and the body. The sleeve stitches will now be held on spare yarn, as you will work the body first. Decreases will be made in the next rnd, since you will no longer be working in the Twisted Cable Rib Pattern.

The body stitches stay on the circular needle and stitches are cast on at the underarms.
The shapeline cables will be included with the body stitches.

Divide (Decrease) Rnd: Removing markers as you go, *knit to next marker decreasing 18 sts evenly as you go, then knit next 2 sts (68 [72, 76] body stitches stay on the circular needle). Knit to next marker decreasing 13 (14, 14) sts evenly as you go and thread these 49 (52, 56) sts onto a spare piece of yarn for the sleeve; repeat from * once more — 136 (144, 152) sts on circular needle for the body

body

Next Rnd: Place a marker for the beginning of the rnd. *Purl to underarm, cast on 4 (5, 7) sts; repeat from * once more — 144 (154, 166) sts.
Purl two more rnds.

Continue in Stockinette Stitch (knit every rnd) until the sweater measures 11¼ (13¼, 15¼)" from the base of the collar down to the needle or 1¾" shy of the desired length required by the recipient.

Next Rnd (Decrease Rnd): Knit, decreasing 0 (2, 2) sts evenly around — 144 (152, 164) sts.

Lower Ribbing
Next Rnd: Work Rnd 4 of Twisted Cable Rib Pattern. Work Rnds 1–4 of the Twisted Cable Rib Pattern 3 times. Bind off ribwise.

sleeves

Set-up Rnd: Using double pointed needles with RS facing, and starting in the center of the underarm cast on sts, pick up and purl 2 (3, 4) sts from the edge of cast on stitches. Pick up and purl 1 extra st here at the

corner to help close the gap, purl sleeve sts off spare yarn. Pick up and purl 1 extra st here at the corner to help close the gap, pick up and purl 2 (2, 3) sts from underarm cast on sts to center of underarm, place marker — 55 (59, 65) sts.

Purl 2 more rnds.
Knit 4 rnds.

Decrease Rnd: K1 (seamline st), SSK, knit to 2 sts before marker, K2tog.
Knit 7 rnds.
Repeat the last 8 rnds, working Decrease Rnd every 8th rnd (do not decrease to less than 41, 45, 45 sts), until sleeve measures 6¼ (8¼, 10¼)" from the underarm or 1¾" shy of desired length for the recipient of the sweater.

Next Rnd: Knit, decreasing 1 stitch — 40 (44, 44) sts.

cuff
Next Rnd: Work Rnd 4 of Twisted Cable Rib Pattern. Now work Rnds 1–4 of the Twisted Cable Rib Pattern 3 times. Bind off ribwise.

finishing
Sew in ends.

hat
Starting at the Top with I-cord
Using size 6 (4.0 mm) double pointed needles, cast on 3 sts and knit a 16" I-cord. Sew in ends. (See page 5 for I-cord instructions.) Weave the I-cord in and out of the eyelet holes at the top of the hat. Draw up to desired tightness. (Note: If your little recipient has a ponytail, the ponytail could be drawn up through the hole.) Knot each end of the I-cord.
After the last rnd, redistribute the stitches onto two

double pointed needles and knit with a third needle. Mark the beginning of your rnd by putting a safety pin through the first stitch of the rnd.
Now work in the rnd.

NOTE: Redistribute the stitches onto more double pointed needles as you increase and to a 16" (40 cm) circular needle when you can.

Increase Rnd: Work [K1, Inc 1] to end of rnd — 8 sts.
Knit 2 rnds.
Increase Rnd: Work [K1, Inc 1] to end of rnd
— 16 sts.
Knit 2 rnds.
Increase Rnd: Work [K1, Inc 1] to end of rnd
— 32 sts.
Knit 3 rnds.
Increase Rnd: Work [K2, Inc 1] to end of rnd
— 48 sts.
Knit 2 rnds.
Increase Rnd: Increase evenly around to 56 (60, 64) sts.
Next Rnd: Work [K1, P1] to end of rnd.

NOTE: Increases in next rnd are indicated by "M1(p)" or "M1(k)". No holes are created when using M1 increases and they are made purlwise or knitwise in order to work the increased stitches into the pattern as soon as possible.

Next Rnd: *K1, M1(k), P1, M1(p); repeat from * to end of rnd — 112 (120, 128) sts.
Next Rnd: *Twist 2, P2; repeat from * to end of rnd.

Work the Twisted Cable Rib Pattern as follows:
Rnd 1: *K2, P2; repeat from * to end of rnd.
Rnds 2 and 3: Repeat Rnd 1.
Rnd 4: *Twist 2, P2; repeat from * to end of rnd.

Repeat these 4 rnds until hat measures 4½ (5, 5½)" from just below the first "Twist 2" rnd. End after a "Twist 2" rnd. Bind off ribwise.
To complete, tie the I-cord into a loose knot and sew in place on the top of the hat.

top down **ridges**

Starting at the top, work the yoke and then work each of the sleeves as long as your child needs them to be. Knit the body as long as needed and you are done. Knitting this sweater with a size smaller needle than wool calls for makes a sturdier garment.

Style Notes: Knit from the top down with no sewing.

Designer: Deb Gemmell
Experience Level: Beginner

sizes
To fit Child: 1 (2, 4, 6) years

finished measurements
Chest: 24 (26, 28, 30)"
Body Length: 12 (13, 15, 17)"
Sleeve Length: 6½ (8, 10, 12)"

materials
Medium Worsted Weight Yarn (3.5 ounces/
   220 yards, 100 grams/ 203 meters per ball):
    Lime Green 3 (3, 4, 4) balls
Size 6 (4.0 mm) 24" (60 cm) circular needle
4 markers
7 (8, 9, 10) ½-inch buttons

gauge
20 sts = 4" (10 cm) on size 6 (4.0 mm) needle over Garter Stitch or size needed to obtain gauge

begin at the top
With circular needle, cast on 70 (70, 78, 78) sts. Working back and forth on circular needle:
NOTE: (Optional) To keep the Front edges firm, you can slip the first stitch of each row as if to knit. This

would count as your first knit stitch of the row in the instructions.

Knit 4 rows.

Increase Row: (RS) K14 (14, 15, 15), YO, K1, place marker, K1, YO, K6 (6, 8, 8), YO, K1, place marker, K1, YO, K22 (22, 24, 24), YO, K1, place marker, K1, YO, K6 (6, 8, 8), YO, K1, place marker, K1, YO, K14 (14, 15, 15) — 78 (78, 86, 86) sts.

Straight Row: (WS) Knit.

Increase Row: (RS) *Knit to 1 stitch before marker, YO, K1, slip marker, K1, YO; repeat from * 3 more times, knit to end of row.

Straight Row: (WS) Knit.

Buttonhole Row:

For Girls (RS): Work Increase Row as set to last 3 sts, YO, K2tog, K1.

For Boys (RS): K1, K2tog, YO, continue Increase Row as set.

Straight Row: (WS) Knit.

Increase Row: (RS) *Knit to 1 stitch before marker, YO, K1, slip marker, K1, YO; repeat from * 3 more times, knit to end of row.

Straight Row: (WS) Knit.

Repeat last 2 rows 5 (6, 7, 8) more times, working Buttonhole Row every 8 ridges (16 rows), until 142 (150, 166, 174) sts on needle — 9 (10, 11, 12) pairs of YO eyelets showing at each of the shapelines.

Note: Shapelines: two stitches separating the pair of increases which creates the distinctive diagonal line of the raglan yoke.

NOTE: Stitches between markers — Fronts have 24 (25, 27, 28) sts, sleeves have 26 (28, 32, 34) sts, Back has 42 (44, 48, 50) sts.

Next Row: (RS) Knit.
Straight Row: (WS) Knit.

Increase Row: (RS) *Knit to 1 stitch before marker, YO, K1, slip marker, K1, YO; repeat from * 3 more times, knit to end of row.

Straight Row: (WS) Knit.

Repeat last 4 rows 8 (9, 10, 11) more times, continuing to work buttonholes as set, until 214 (230, 254, 270) sts on needle — 18 (20, 22, 24) pairs of YO eyelets showing at each of the shapelines.

NOTE: Stitches between markers — Fronts have 33 (35, 38, 40) sts each, both of the sleeves have 44 (48, 54, 58) sts and the Back has 60 (64, 70, 74) sts.

Knit 4 rows.

sleeves

Set-Up Row: (RS) Knit 33 (35, 38, 40) sts of Front, knit 44 (48, 54, 58) sts of sleeve, leaving the rest of the sts on the needle unworked, turn.

First Sleeve

Next Row: (WS) Knit 44 (48, 54, 58) sts for sleeve, turn — 1 ridge on sleeve.

Working back and forth on 44 (48, 54, 58) sts of sleeve:

Knit 6 rows — 4 ridges on RS of sleeve.

Decrease Row: K1, SSK, knit to last 3 sts, K2tog, K1.

Knit 7 rows.

Repeat last 8 rows until sleeve measures 4½ (6, 8, 10)" long. Do not decrease to less than 34 (34, 36, 36) sts.

Next Row: Knit, decreasing to 34 (34, 36, 36) sts if necessary.

Knit every row for 2" more, ending with a RS row. (Sleeve length is now 6½ [8, 10, 12]" long.)

Bind off on WS row.

Second Sleeve

Attach yarn and knit 60 (64, 70, 74) sts of Back, knit 44 (48, 54, 58) sts of second sleeve, turn.

Work as for first sleeve above.

body

Attach yarn and knit 33 (35, 38, 40) sts of Front — 126 (134, 146, 154) sts on circular needle for body.

Knit every row, continuing to work buttonholes as set, until body measures 11 (12, 14, 16)" from cast on edge at neck.

Decrease Row: K5, K2tog, K23 (25, 28, 30), K2tog, K2, K2tog, K26 (28, 31, 33), K2tog, K26 (28, 31, 33), K2tog, K2, K2tog, K23 (25, 28, 30), K2tog, K5 — 119 (127, 139, 147) sts.

Knit every row for 1" more or to desired length, ending with RS row.

Bind off with WS facing.

finishing

Sew on buttons and sew in ends.

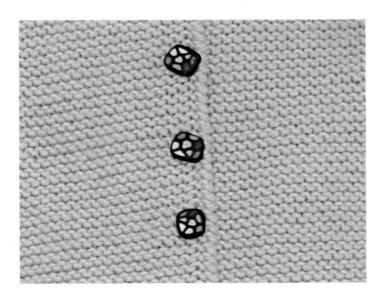

51

one piece &
cuff-to-cuff
sweaters

one piece

Another favorite with "Heck no, we won't sew!" knitters, this traditional knitting "in one piece" method is ideal for many types of pullovers, cardigans, tops, and vests.

With pullovers, you begin at the bottom of the garment and work "in the round" to the underarm, knitting the front and back of the body at the same time. The yoke is worked back and forth with the garment still in one piece. Shoulders are joined, usually by a 3-Needle Bind Off (or sew the seams, if you're not as anti-sew as we are), and then the sleeves are picked up and knit down from the shoulders to the wrist for the perfect sleeve length. Cardigans and vests are worked back and forth in one piece, from the bottom to the underarm, with the two fronts and back worked individually then joined in the same way as pullovers.

In the following pages you'll find easy vests, a cropped top, cardigans and pullovers to try out. For the more advanced knitter, there is a fabulous Fair Isle and and an oh-so-special Chanel style jacket for your little fashion diva!

work from the cuff

Sometimes it's worth it to sew!
The exception to our one piece rule is this interesting and fun sweater jacket. It's worked in two pieces and joined up the center back. Working towards the middle from each cuff makes it easy to fashion vertical stripes in easy garter stitch, and you can play with different light/dark color schemes.

daddy's little helper
jean jacket

I designed this garment for my little boy who was just starting school for the first time. I took Daddy's favorite jean jacket and fashioned "faux" seams in appropriate places on the scaled down garment. My youngest daughter wanted one, too. For her I knit the collar and cuffs in a fancy boucle and used more elaborate buttons.

Style Notes: Knit in one piece, from the bottom up. Sleeves are picked up and knit from the shoulders down to the wrist. You have the choice of a real pocket or a faux pocket. Some sewing required.

Designer: Anne Russell
Experience Level: Intermediate

sizes
To fit Child: 1 (2, 4, 6) years

finished measurements
Chest: 24 (26, 28, 30)"
Body Length: 12 (13, 15, 17)"
Sleeve Length: 6½ (8, 10, 12)"

materials
DK, Light Weight Yarn (3.5 ounces/250 yards,
   100 grams/230 meters per ball):
      Light Blue 2 (3, 3, 4) balls
Size 3 (3.25 mm) 24" (60 cm) circular needle
Size 6 (4.0 mm) 24" (60 cm) circular needle
Set of size 3 (3.25 mm) double pointed needles
Set of size 6 (4.0 mm) double pointed needles
6 (6, 8, 8) ¾-inch silver toned buttons

gauge
22 sts = 4" (10 cm) on size 6 (4.00 mm) or size needed to obtain gauge

to begin

With smaller circular needle, cast on 132 (144, 156, 164) sts.

Border:

With WS facing, purl 1 row.

Knit 9 (9, 11, 13) rows (with RS showing 4 [4, 5, 6] ridges), ending after a RS row.

Starting with WS facing, purl 3 rows, ending after WS row.

body

Change to larger circular needle and set up faux seams.

Row 1: (RS) K15 (16, 18, 19), P1, K1, P1, K30 (33, 36, 38), P1, K1, P1, K30 (34, 36, 38), P1, K1, P1, K30 (33, 36, 38), P1, K1, P1, K15 (16, 18, 19).

Row 2: P15 (16, 18, 19), K1, P1, K1, P30 (33, 36, 38), K1, P1, K1, P30 (34, 36, 38), K1, P1, K1, P30 (33, 36, 38), K1, P1, K1, P15 (16, 18, 19).

Repeat last 2 rows until work measures 6 (6, 7½, 9)" from cast on edge, ending after a WS row.

Divide for Armholes

With RS facing, work in pattern as set for 32 (35, 38, 40) sts, bind off 2 sts, work 64 (70, 76, 80) sts (including st on right needle after bind off), bind off 2 sts, continue in pattern to end of row.

NOTE: Your needle has 32 (35, 38, 40) sts, armhole gap, 64 (70, 76, 80) sts, armhole gap, 32 (35, 38, 40) sts.

Work Left Front first, place the Back and Right Front stitches on a spare piece of yarn or spare circular needle.

left front

With WS facing, work across 32 (35, 38, 40) sts of Left Front in pattern as set for 3 rows, ending after a WS row.

Set Up Pocket

Row 1: K7 (8, 10, 11), P19, K6 (8, 9, 10).

Row 2: P6 (8, 9, 10), K1, P17, K1, P7 (8, 10, 11).

Row 3: K7 (8, 10, 11), P1, K1, P15, K1, P1, K6 (8, 9, 10).

Row 4: P6 (8, 9, 10), K1, P1, K1, P13, K1, P1, K1, P7 (8, 10, 11).

Pocket Outline Pattern

Pocket Pattern Row 1: (RS) K7 (8, 10, 11), P1, K1, P1, K13, P1, K1, P1, K6 (8, 9, 10).

Pocket Pattern Row 2: (WS) P6 (8, 9, 10), K1, P1, K1, P13, K1, P1, K1, P7 (8, 10, 11).

Repeat Pocket Pattern Rows 1 and 2 until sweater measures 8 (8½, 10, 11½)" from cast on edge.

Horizontal Seam

Next Row: (RS) P7 (8, 10, 11), P1, K1, P1, K13, P1, K1, P1, P6 (8, 9, 10).
Next Row: (WS) P6 (8, 9, 10), K1, P1, K1, P13, K1, P1, K1, P7 (8, 10, 11).
Next Row: (RS) K7 (8, 10, 11), P1, K1, P1, K13, P1, K1, P1, K6 (8, 9, 10).
Next Row: (WS) K6 (8, 9, 10), K1, P1, K1, P13, K1, P1, K1, K7 (8, 10, 11).

Continue repeating Pocket Outline Pattern Rows 1 and 2 above until pocket outline is 3" deep, measured from second ridge of pocket.

Pocket Options – Real Pocket or Faux Pocket
Real Pocket:
Next Row: With RS facing, K7 (8, 10, 11), P1, K1, P1, bind off 13 sts for pocket opening, work to end of row in pattern as set.
Next Row: Purl across row, casting on 13 stitches over pocket opening — 32 (35, 38, 40) sts.
OR
Faux Pocket:
Next Row: With RS facing, K7 (8, 10, 11), P1, K1, P1, purl across 13 sts of pocket, P1, K1, P1, K6 (8, 9, 10) sts.
Next Row: Purl.

Work even in Stockinette Stitch until Left Front measures 10 (10½, 13, 15)", ending with a RS row so that you are at the neck edge.

Neck Shaping
With WS facing, bind off 8 sts at neck edge, purl to end of row.

Continue in Stockinette Stitch, decreasing 1 stitch at neck edge every other row, 5 times — 19 (22, 25, 27) sts.
Continue in Stockinette Stitch until Front measures 12 (13, 15, 17)" from cast on edge, ending with a WS row.
Purl 2 rows. Place stitches on holder.

back
With WS facing, join yarn to 64 (70, 76, 80) sts for Back, work in pattern as set until Back measures 8 (8½, 10, 11½)" from cast on edge, ending after a WS row.

Horizontal Seam
Beginning with RS facing, purl 2 rows.
Knit 2 rows.

Work in Stockinette Stitch until Back measures 12 (13, 15, 17)" from cast on edge, ending after a WS row.
Purl 2 rows. Place stitches on stitch holder.

right front
With WS facing, join yarn at underarm and continue in pattern as set until Front measures 8 (8½, 10, 11½)" from cast on edge, ending after a WS row.

Horizontal Seam
Beginning with RS facing, purl 2 rows.
Knit 2 rows.

Work in Stockinette Stitch until Right Front measures 10 (10½, 13, 15)" from cast on edge, ending after a WS row.

Begin Neck Shaping
Next Row: (RS) At neck edge, bind off 8 sts, knit to end of row.

Continue to work in Stockinette Stitch, decreasing 1 stitch at neck edge every other row, 5 times — 19 (22, 25, 27) sts.

Continue even in Stockinette Stitch until Front measures 12 (13, 15, 17)", ending after a WS row.
Purl 2 rows.

Join shoulders using 3-Needle Bind Off with RS facing OR bind off shoulder stitches on Fronts and same number of shoulder stitches at beginning and end of Back and sew shoulders together. You should have 26 stitches for back of neck stitches left on the holder.

sleeves (both the same)

With larger double pointed needles, pick up and knit 1 stitch in the second bind off stitch at the underarm. Pick up and knit 3 stitches for every 4 rows around armhole edges, pick up and knit 1 stitch in the first bind off stitch at underarm, place marker to mark the end of the rnd — approximately 68 (78, 84, 90) sts.
Work in the round:
Knit every rnd for 1".

Decrease Round: SSK, knit to last 2 sts, K2tog.
Knit 1 (1, 2, 2) rnds.
Repeat last 2 (2, 3, 3) rnds until sleeve measures 5 (6½, 8, 10)". Do not decrease to less than 34 (36, 44, 44) sts. If necessary, work even to desired length.

cuff: all sizes

Change to smaller double-pointed needles.
Purl 1 round, decreasing if necessary to 34 (36, 44, 44) sts.
Knit 2 rnds.
Purl 1 rnd.
Rnd 1: Knit.

Rnd 2: Purl
Repeat Rnds 1 and 2, 2 (2, 3, 4) more times.
Knit 2 rnds.
Bind off purlwise, very loosely.

finishing

Right Front Button Band

With smaller circular needle and RS facing, starting at bottom, pick up and knit 3 sts for every 4 rows up right Front edge.
Work back and forth on circular needle:
Starting with the WS facing, knit 2 rows.
Purl 5 (5, 7, 7) rows.
Knit 1 row.
With WS facing, bind off knitwise.
Using waste yarn, make a mark in 5 (5, 7, 7) places for buttons on Right Front, with first and last button placed 1" from either end, and the remaining 3 (3, 5, 5) buttons evenly spaced on the rest of the button band.

Left Front Buttonhole Band

With smaller circular needle, RS facing, and starting at top, pick up and knit 3 sts for every 4 rows down Left Front edge.
Work back and forth on circular needle:
Starting with WS facing, knit 2 rows.
Purl 2 (2, 4, 4) rows.
Place Buttonholes: With WS facing, purl, making buttonholes to match the button markers on the Right Front by binding off 2 sts.
Finish Buttonholes: Purl, casting on 2 sts to close buttonholes.
Purl 1 row.
Knit 1 row.
With WS facing, bind off knitwise.
Sew buttons on Right Front button band.

Shaped Collar

Row 1: With smaller-sized circular needle or double pointed needles and RS of sweater facing, starting at Right Front (do not pick up stitches from the button band) pick up and knit 8 sts along Right Front neck bind off. Pick up and knit 3 sts for every 4 rows along neck shaping to top of shoulder, knit 26 sts from back of neck, pick up and knit 3 sts for every 4 rows down Left Front neck shaping, pick up and knit 8 sts across left neck bind off stitches, turn.

Work back and forth as follows:

Row 2: (WS) Knit.

Row 3: K1, P1, knit to last 2 sts, P1, K1.

Row 4: P1, K1, P1, M1, purl to last 3 sts, M1, P1, K1, P1.

Row 5: (RS) K1, P1, knit to last 2 sts, P1, K1.

Row 6: P1, K1, P1, M1, knit to last 3 sts, M1, P1, K1, P1.

Repeat Rows 5 and 6 above 4 (4, 5, 6) more times, ending after a WS row.

Next Row: K1, P1, K1, purl to last 3 sts, K1, P1, K1. With WS of sweater facing and larger needle, bind off loosely purlwise.

Collar is flipped over when worn so WS rows above are showing.

Pocket Finishing

Faux Pocket: If you did not bind off sts for the pocket opening on the Left Front, work pocket tab below ONLY, and do not complete pocket trim or pocket lining.

Pocket Tab (Real and Faux Pockets)

Cast on 19 stitches.

(RS) Purl 1 row.

Knit 2 rows.

Purl 1 row.

Knit 4 rows.

Knit, decreasing 1 stitch at beginning and end of row — 17 sts.

Knit.

Knit, decreasing 1 stitch at beginning and end of row — 15 sts.

Knit.

Buttonhole Row: Knit 6, bind off 3 sts, knit to end of row.

K6, cast on 3 sts to close buttonhole, K6 — 15 sts.

Knit, decreasing 1 stitch at beginning and end of row — 13 sts.

Knit.

Knit, decreasing 1 stitch at beginning and end of row — 11 sts.

Knit.

Bind off all stitches.

Sew the pocket tab onto Left Front 1 or 2 rows above pocket trim (for faux pocket sew tab onto Left Front 1 or 2 rows above purled sts at top of pocket), so that the pocket tab folds down on top of pocket. Sew button to line up with buttonhole, (for Faux Pocket sew button through pocket tab and fabric of Front).

Pocket Trim (Real Pocket Only)

With smaller double pointed needles and RS facing, pick up and knit 13 sts from bind off edge of pocket on Left Front.

Knit 3 rows.

Bind off loosely. Tack down side edges of pocket trim.

Pocket Lining (Real Pocket Only)

With larger double pointed needles and RS facing, pick up and knit 13 sts from cast on edge at top of pocket. Working down, knit in Stockinette Stitch for 3". Bind off. Sew pocket lining to WS of Left Front loosely.

the cameron

I wanted to knit a sweater with slightly rounded shoulders produced by the increases in the ribbed yoke. The style is ageless and when knit in a good quality yarn, wool or cotton, this sweater is sure to be passed down and worn lovingly by more than one little girl or boy.

Style Notes: Knit in the round, from the bottom up in one piece. Sleeves picked up and knit from the shoulders down to the wrists. No sewing required.

Designer: Bernice Vollick
Experience Level: Beginner/Intermediate

sizes
To fit Child: 1 (2, 4, 6) years
Chest Measurement: 20 (22, 24, 26)"

finished measurements
Chest: 24 (26, 28, 30)"
Body Length: 12 (13, 15, 17)"
Sleeve Length: 6½ (8, 10, 12)"

materials
Worsted Weight Yarn (3.5 ounces/220 yards,
    100 grams/203 meters per ball):
        Navy Blue (MC) 3 (3, 4, 4)
        Mint Green (CC) 1 (1, 1, 1)
Size 7 (4.5 mm) 16" (40 cm) circular needle
Size 7 (4.5 mm) 24" (60 cm) circular needle
Set of size 7 (4.5 mm) double pointed needles for
    sleeves and neckline
Size 8 (5.0 mm) 16" (40 cm) circular needle to
    cast on bottom edge and neckband bind off for a
    looser edge.
2 markers of different colors to label beginning of rnd

gauge

20 stitches = 4" (10 cm) using size 7 (4.5 mm) needle or size needed to obtain gauge

begin with the rib

With MC and larger circular needle, cast on 108 (116, 124, 136) sts.

Join in the rnd, being careful not to twist your stitches.

Rnd 1: Place marker for beginning of rnd and work [K2, P2] rib to end of rnd.

Change to size 7 (4.5 mm) 24" (60 cm) circular needle.

Work [K2, P2] ribbing as established for 1½ (1½, 2, 2)".

body

Rnd 1: Knit, increasing 14 (12, 16, 16) sts evenly around — 122 (128, 140, 152) sts.

Rnd 2: Purl.

Rnd 3: Knit.

Knit every rnd until work measures 2 (2, 3, 3¾)" from cast on edge.

Stripe Pattern

Knit every rnd, changing colors as indicated:

2 rnds in CC, 3 rnds in MC, 5 rnds in CC, 8 rnds in MC, 5 rnds in CC, 3 rnds in MC, 2 rnds in CC.

Break CC.

Continue knitting every rnd in MC until work measures 7 (7½, 8½, 9½)" from cast on edge or desired length to underarm.

Next Rnd: Purl.

Next Rnd: K61 (64, 70, 76), place second marker, knit to end of rnd. Note: Each marker placed at the center underarm.

Separate work for Front and Back: K3, P1, work [K2, P1] to 3 stitches before the underarm marker, K3; place remaining stitches on a stitch holder or thread a spare piece of yarn through the remaining stitches, turn — 61 (64, 70, 76) sts left on needle.

back

Working back and forth on circular needle:

Next Row: With WS facing, P3, K1, work [P2, K1] to last three stitches, P3, turn — 61 (64, 70, 76) sts.

Row 1: (RS) K3, P1, K1, M1, K1, P1, work [K2, P1] to last 6 stitches, K1, M1, K1, P1, K3, turn — 63 (66, 72, 78) sts.

Row 2: P3, K1, P3, K1, work [P2, K1] to last 7 stitches, P3, K1, P3, turn.

Row 3: (RS) K3, P1, K1, M1, K1, M1, K1, P1, work [K2, P1] to last 7 stitches, K1, M1, K1, M1, K1, P1, K3, turn — 67 (70, 76, 82) sts.

Row 4: P3, K1, work [P2, K1] to last 3 stitches, P3, turn.

Row 5: (RS) K3, P1, work [K2, P1] to last 3 stitches, K3, turn.

Row 6: P3, K1, work [P2, K1] to last 3 stitches, P3, turn.

Repeat Rows 1–6, 1 (2, 3, 3) more times — 73 (82, 94, 100) sts on the needle.

Repeat Rows 5 and 6 until work measures 5½ (6½, 7, 7½)" from underarm, ending with a WS row. Place Back stitches on a stitch holder or a contrasting piece of yarn.

front

Place Front stitches on a size 7 (4.5 mm) 24" (60 cm) circular needle and with RS facing, K3, P1, work [K2, P1] to last 3 sts, K3 — 61 (64, 70, 76) sts.

Next Row: With WS facing, P3, K1 work [P2, K1] to last 3 stitches, P3, turn — 61 (64, 70, 76) sts.

Work Rows 1–6 as for Back until there are 73 (82, 94, 100) sts on the needle.

Repeat Rows 5 and 6 until work measures 3½ (4, 4½, 4½)" from underarm, ending with a WS row, turn.

Work sides of neck, working both shoulders at same time:

With RS facing, work 24 (27, 30, 33) sts in the rib pattern as set, K1, place the next 23 (26, 32, 32) sts on a stitch holder or piece of contrasting yarn for front of neck. Join in another ball of MC for second shoulder, K1, work next 24 (27, 30, 33) sts in the rib pattern as set, turn — 25 (28, 31, 34) sts for each shoulder.

NOTE: On RS rows, shoulders will begin and end with a K3, and WS rows will begin and end with P3. Continue to work back and forth in pattern as established, working both sides of the neckline at the same time, until work measures 5½ (6½ , 7, 7½)" from underarm to match the Back, ending with a WS row.

Join Shoulders

Place the first 25 (28, 31, 34) sts of the Back onto a double pointed needle, hold Front and Back shoulders together with RS facing, bind off the Front and Back shoulders using 3–Needle Bind Off. Repeat for the second shoulder.

neckband

Place the remaining 23 (26, 32, 32) Center Back stitches on the smaller 16" circular needle.
With Back of sweater facing, join in MC at right shoulder neck edge and knit across the 23 (26, 32, 32) back of neck stitches, pick up and K9 (12, 12, 14) sts down Left Front neck edge, K23 (26, 32, 32) front neck stitches, pick up and K9 (12, 12, 14) sts up Right Front neck edge, place marker at the beginning of the

rnd — 64 (76, 88, 92) sts on the needle.

Rnd 1: Purl.
Rnd 2: Knit.
Rnd 3: Work [K2, P2] to end of rnd.
Repeat [K2, P2] rib as established until ribbing measures 1½".
Bind off in ribbing using the larger circular needle to avoid making the neck opening too tight.

sleeves

With MC and double pointed needles, pick up and knit 1 stitch at the bottom center of the armhole between the Front and Back yokes, pick up and K50 (56, 62, 70) sts evenly around the armhole opening. Divide 51 (57, 63, 71) sts evenly among needles and mark the beginning center stitch with a safety pin. (This center stitch will be the center seam line stitch for the decreasing of the sleeves.)

Double Decrease Rnd: Knit around sleeve to 1 stitch before the marked center underarm stitch, SL2 (k)–K1-P2SSO.
Knit next 4 (4, 5, 5) rnds.
Repeat last 5 (5, 6, 6) rnds 4 (5, 6, 8) times more — 41 (45, 49, 53) sts.
Continue to knit every rnd with no further decreases until sleeve measures 5 (6½ , 8, 10)" from underarm, or desired length before cuff.

cuff

Rnd 1: Purl.
Rnd 2: Knit, decrease to 40 (44, 48, 52) sts.
Rnd 3: Work [K2, P2] to end of rnd.
Continue to work [K2, P2] rib as established until cuff measures 1½ (1½, 2, 2)".
Bind off in ribbing using the larger needle.

sam's delight

This pattern was designed to be comfy and roomy for the active boy or girl. The broken rib stitch gives this sweater a ribbed look without the cling. The result is a loose fitting pullover that can easily double as a jacket for those cool days of late fall or early spring. Cozy and warm, this pattern truly is "Sam's Delight."

Style Notes: Knit in Garter Stitch top down (but not a raglan). No sewing required.

Designer: Bernice Vollick
Experience Level: Intermediate

sizes
To fit Child: 1 (2, 4, 6) years

finished measurements
Chest: 24 (26, 28 30)"
Body Length: 13 (14, 16, 18)"
Sleeve Length: 6½ (8, 10, 12)" without trim

materials
Worsted Weight Yarn (3.5 ounces/220 yards,
    100 grams/203 meters per ball):
        Blue (A) 2 (2, 2, 3) balls
        Red (B) 1 (1, 2, 2) balls
Size 8 (5.0 mm) 16" (40 cm) circular needle
Size 7 (4.5 mm) 16" (40 cm) circular needle
Size 7 (4.5 mm) 24" (60 cm) circular needle
Set of size 7 (4.5 mm) double point needles
Stitch holders or spare yarn to thread through
    stitches to be held

gauge
20 sts = 4" (10 cm) with size 7 (4.5 mm) needles in Stockinette Stitch or size needed to obtain gauge

begin at neckband

With larger circular needle and B, cast on 64 (72, 80, 88) sts. Join in a circle, being careful not to twist stitches and place marker for beginning of rnd.
Work [K2, P2] ribbing to end of rnd.
Change to size 7 (4.5 mm) 16" (40 cm) circular needle and work [K2, P2] ribbing as established until neckband measures 1 (1½, 1½, 1½)" from cast on edge.

Next Rnd: Knit, increasing or decreasing as indicated for size, +2 (+2, −2, +2) stitches evenly around — 66 (74, 78, 90) sts.
Next Rnd: Purl. Mark RS of neckband with safety pin.
NOTE: It is important to mark the RS, as the ribbing of the neckband and the Garter Stitch panels to follow both look the same on the RS and the WS.

right shoulder panel

With RS facing and one double pointed needle, K11 (13, 13, 15), leaving remaining sts of neckband on circular needle to be held for later.
Using 2 double pointed needles:
Turn and K11 (13, 13, 15) for right shoulder.
Knit every row for 33 (37, 41, 43) rows, ending with a RS row. Note: On RS you should be able to count 18 (20, 22, 23) Garter Stitch ridges including the last purl row before separating the stitches for the shoulder as the first ridge in the shoulder panel.
Place 11 (13, 13, 15) sts on a stitch holder or spare piece of yarn. Break B.

left shoulder panel

With RS facing, place next 22 (24, 26, 30) sts on stitch holder or spare piece of yarn to be held for the yoke front.
With RS facing and using one double pointed needle, reattach B, and knit the next 11 (13, 13, 15) sts for left shoulder.

Work as right shoulder, ending with a RS row. **Do not break yarn.** Place the 11 (13, 13, 15) sts from the left shoulder panel on a stitch holder or spare piece of yarn.

yoke back

Turn the left shoulder panel. With same yarn and longer circular needle (24") and with RS facing, pick up and knit 18 (20, 22, 23) sts along the side of the left shoulder panel (1 stitch for every ridge). Knit 22 (24, 26, 30) sts off of the short circular needle for back of neck. Pick up and knit 18 (20, 22, 23) sts along the side of the right shoulder panel (1 stitch for every ridge) — 58 (64, 70, 76) sts on the long circular needle.

Work back and forth on circular needle:
Knit every row for 41 (45, 51, 55) rows. Note: On RS you should be able to count 21 (23, 26, 28) ridges from shoulder panel. Do not include the last purl rnd at the neckband, ending after a WS row.
Place stitches on a spare circular needle. Break yarn.

yoke front

With longer circular needle (24") and with RS facing, pick up and knit 18 (20, 22, 23) sts along the side of right shoulder panel (1 stitch for every ridge). Place the 22 (24, 26, 30) sts from the front of the neckband on a double pointed needle and knit, pick up and knit 18 (20, 22, 23) sts (1 stitch for every ridge) along the side of the left shoulder panel — 58 (64, 70, 76) sts on circular needle.

Work back and forth on circular needle:
Knit every row for 41 (45, 51, 55) rows to match Back, ending with a WS row. Break yarn — 21 (23, 26, 28) ridges showing on the RS.

body

Turn the yoke front so you have the RS facing, attach A. Cast on 1 stitch, knit the cast-on st, and knit across Front 29 (32, 35, 38) sts, M1, K29 (32, 35, 38) sts, and with same circular needle, cast on 1 stitch, knit across the back yoke sts from spare circular needle as follows: K29 (32, 35, 38) sts, M1, K29 (32, 35, 38) sts. Join in the rnd and place marker for beginning of rnd — 120 (132, 144, 156) sts on circular needle.

Working in round:
Rnd 1: K3, P1, work [K5, P1] to last 2 sts of rnd, K2 — 120 (132, 144, 156) sts on circular needle.
Rnd 2: Knit to end of rnd.
Rnd 3: K3, P1, work [K5, P1] to last 2 sts, K2.
Repeat last 2 rnds until body in A measures 7 (7½, 8½, 9½)", ending with Rnd 3. Break A.

trim

Rnd 1: With B, knit to end of rnd, decreasing 12 stitches evenly in the rnd — 108 (120, 132, 144) sts on the needle.
Rnd 2: Purl.
Rnd 3: Knit.
Rnd 4: Purl.
Repeat Rnds 3 and 4 once more. Note: On RS you should have 3 Garter Stitch ridges.
Bind off knitwise.

sleeves

On RS using size 7 (4.5 mm) 16" (40 cm) circular needle, attach A at the center of underarm. Pick up and K1 stitch at the center underarm, pick up and K21 (23, 26, 28) sts along the side of yoke (1 stitch for every ridge), place the shoulder panel stitches on a spare double pointed needle and knit across 11 (13, 13, 15) panel sts, pick up and K21 (23, 26, 28) sts along the side of the yoke (1 stitch for every ridge) — 54 (60, 66, 72) sts.

NOTE: The first stitch in the rnd will become the center underarm stitch for the double decrease. Mark this first stitch with a safety pin, re-pinning it after working every decrease.

Rnd 1: Knit to end of rnd.
Rnd 2: K3, P1, work [K5, P1] to last 2 sts in the rnd, K2.
Repeat the last two rnds once more.
Double Decrease Rnd: Knit around sleeve to 1 stitch before the marked center underarm st, SL2(k)-K1-P2SSO, re-pinning the safety pin marker into the decreased stitch.

Continue with pattern as set, work a Decrease Rnd every 4th rnd until sleeve measures 6½ (8, 10, 12)" from underarm. Do not decrease to less than 36 (36, 42, 42) sts. If necessary, work even in pattern to desired length. Break yarn.

Sleeve Trim
Rnd 1: With B, knit, if necessary decrease to 36 (36, 42, 42) sts.
Rnd 2: Purl.
Rnd 3: Knit.
Rnd 4: Purl.
Repeat last 2 rnds once more.
NOTE: On RS you should be able to count 3 Garter Stitch ridges.
Bind off knitwise.

sherbet stripes
hoodie sweater

• •

This hooded cardigan with its colorful stripes and minimal shaping is an easy project. Let your child pick favorite colors or let it be a surprise. You can color this sweater in as few or as many different color stripes as you wish. It would also look great in a main color with only one contrast color.

Style Notes: Knit in one piece, from the bottom up. Work the body of the sweater, including the button bands, back and forth in one piece to the armholes. Then divide for the 2 Fronts and the Back, which are worked separately, also back and forth. After joining the shoulders, knit the hood to the top. Pick up the sleeves at the armhole edge and knit in the round down to the cuff. I suggest weaving in ends as you go, so to finish just sew on buttons and your hoodie is ready for that special child to wear.

Designer: Dana Gibbons
Experience Level: Enthusiastic Beginner

sizes
To fit Child: 1 (2, 4, 6) years

finished measurements
Chest: 24 (26, 28, 30)"
Body Length: 12, (14, 14, 16)"
Sleeve Length: 6½, (8, 10, 12)"

materials
DK, Light Worsted Weight Yarn (3.5 ounces/250 yards, 100 grams/230 meters per ball):
    White (MC) 3 (3, 3, 4) balls
    Green (CC1), Yellow (CC2), Purple (CC3), Pink (CC4), Blue (CC3) ½ (½, ½, ½) ball for each CC
Size 5 (3.75 mm) 24" (60 cm) circular needle OR pair of straight needles

Size 5 (3.75 mm) 16" (40 cm) circular needle
   (optional but recommended for sleeves)
Size 3 (3.25 mm) 24" (60 cm) circular needle OR
   pair of straight needles
Set of size 5 (3.75 mm) double pointed needles
Set of size 3 (3.25 mm) double pointed needles
5 (6, 7, 8) ½-inch shank buttons in several colors to
   match CC OR all one color to match MC
5 (6, 7, 8) small shirt buttons
Buttonhole twist craft thread (color for sewing
   on buttons)
2 markers
2 small safety pins or stitch holders
3 larger stitch holders or spare needles for holding
   non-working stitches

gauge

22 sts = 4" (10 cm) on size 5 (3.75 mm) in Garter
Stitch or size needed to obtain gauge
10 rows in Garter Rib Pattern = 1"

garter stitch rib pattern

Row 1: With CC knit.
Row 2: With CC purl.
Rows 3 and 4: Repeat Rows 1 and 2.
Rows 5–10: With MC, knit (makes 3 ridges on RS).
Repeat 10 rows.

For multicolored stripes, change color with each
repeat, in the following sequence:
Green (CC1), Yellow (CC2), Purple (CC3), Pink (CC4),
Blue (CC5).

let's begin

NOTE: Place buttonholes on both the right and left
button bands. The buttons and buttonholes will line
up perfectly when you sew the buttons over the holes
on the appropriate button band.

With size 3 (3.25 mm) 24" (60 cm) circular or straight
needles and MC, cast on 136 (152, 164, 176) sts.
Working back and forth:
Starting on the WS, Knit 9 (9, 11, 11) rows — 5 (5, 6,
6) Garter Stitch ridges showing on RS with cast on
row counted as first ridge.

NOTE: Do not cut the MC but carry it up the sides
loosely as you work.
Row 1: (RS) With larger circular or straight needles
and CC1, K5, place marker, knit to last 5 sts, place
marker, K5.
Row 2: K5, slip marker, purl to next marker, slip
marker, K5.
Row 3 (Buttonholes): (RS) Continuing with CC1, K1,
K2tog, YO, K2, slip marker, knit to next marker, slip
marker, K2, YO, K2tog, K1.
Row 4: K5, purl to last 5 sts, K5. Cut CC1, leaving a
3" tail for weaving in. (Buttonhole sits between 2
Garter Stitch ridges.)
Rows 5–10: With MC, knit every row, do not cut MC
— makes 3 ridges on RS.
Row 11: (RS) With CC2, knit.
Row 12: K5, purl to last 5 sts, K5.
Row 13: Knit.
Row 14: K5, purl to last 5 sts, K5. Cut CC2.
Row 15–20: With MC, knit every row.

Work the 10 rows of the Garter Stitch Rib Pattern,
maintaining the button bands at the Front edges in
Garter Stitch as set and **at the same time** placing
buttonholes in every second CC band as above. Work
until you have 6 (7, 7, 8) CC bands, ending with Row
10 (MC).

Divide for Right Front

Row 1: (RS) With next color in sequence, K35
(40, 43, 46) sts, turn. Leave remaining stitches on a

spare needle or stitch holder.

Row 2: Purl to last 5 sts, K5.

Row 3: Knit, (placing buttonhole if necessary).

Row 4: Purl to last 5 sts, K5.

Continue working Garter Rib Pattern as set, maintaining button band on Right Front edge, placing buttonholes every second color band as established until 5 (6, 6, 7) more CC stripes have been worked, ending with Row 4 (stripe with buttonhole).

Decrease for Neck Edge: Do not make any more buttonholes.

Next Row: (RS) With MC, K5, slip marker, K1, SSK, knit to end of row.

Next Row: (WS) Knit.

Repeat last 2 rows twice more — 32 (37, 40, 43) sts. Change to next CC:

Next Row: K5, slip marker, K1, SSK, knit to end of row.

Next Row: Purl to last 5 sts, slip marker, K5.

Repeat last 2 rows once more — 30 (35, 38, 41) sts. With MC, knit 6 rows.

Place these stitches on a stitch holder or spare needle.

Divide for Back

Return to stitches placed on first holder.

With RS facing, put first 2 sts from holder onto a safety pin for armhole, reattach next CC, K62 (68, 74, 80) sts from holder, turn. Leave rest of stitches on holder for Left Front.

Next Row: Purl.

Next Row: Knit.

Next Row: Purl.

Continue to work Garter Stitch Rib Pattern until Back measures the same as the Right Front.

Joining Right Front to right shoulder of Back:

Slip stitches of Right Front onto a larger double point-ed needle. With RS facing, start at armhole edge, work 3-Needle Bind Off on WS of work, binding off 18 (20, 22, 24) sts. Break yarn and pull through stitch on right needle. Note: Leave all the remaining stitches on both of the needles on hold for hood; keep the marker in place.

Return to body of sweater to finish Left Front.

Left Front

With RS facing, put first 2 sts on safety pin for armhole, reattach next CC, knit to end of row, turn.

Next Row: K5, slip marker, purl to end of row. Continue Garter Stitch Rib Pattern, maintaining button band and continue to place buttonholes as set. Work until 5 (6, 6, 7) more CC stripes have been worked, ending with Row 4 (CC stripe with buttonhole).

Decrease for Neck Edge: Do not make any more buttonholes.

Next Row: (RS) With MC, knit to last 8 sts, K2tog, K1, slip marker, K5.

Next Row: Knit.

Repeat last 2 rows twice more — 32 (37, 40, 43) sts.

Next Row: With appropriate CC, knit to last 8 sts, K2tog, K1, slip marker, K5.

Next Row: K5, purl to end.

Repeat last 2 rows once more — 30 (35, 38, 41) sts. With MC, knit 6 rows.

Joining Left Front to left shoulder of Back:

With RS of Left Front and left shoulder of Back facing, starting at armhole edge, work 3-Needle Bind Off on WS, binding off 18 (20, 22, 24) sts. Note: Leave all the remaining stitches on both of the needles on hold for hood; keep the marker in place. You are now going to continue knitting these stitches for the hood.

hood

On RS with size 5 (3.75 cm) circular needle and next CC in the sequence, starting at Right Front K11 (14, 15, 16) sts from Right Front, pick up and K2 sts from shoulder join to close the gap, K24 (26, 28, 30) sts from back of neck, pick up and K2 sts to close gap at left shoulder, K11 (14, 15, 16) sts from Left Front, turn — 50 (58, 62, 66) sts.

Next Row (WS): K5, slip marker, purl to next marker, slip marker, K5.

Next Row: K6, *M1, K2; repeat from * to last 4 sts, K4 — 70 (82, 88, 94) sts.

Next Row: K5, slip marker, purl to last 5 sts, slip marker, K5.

Continue even in Garter Rib Pattern as set, maintaining Garter Stitch bands at each end (do not make buttonholes), until hood measures 7 (7½, 8, 9)" or desired length from Increase Row, ending with Row 4 or Row 10 of Garter Rib Pattern.

Place half of stitches on the smaller circular needle. Working from front of hood, with RS facing, work 3-Needle Bind Off on all sts.

sleeves

Pick up stitches at the armhole edge and knit sleeve in the round down to the cuff. Use a size 5 (3.75 mm) 16" (40 cm) circular needle until sleeve becomes too narrow then change to double pointed needles.

With RS of work facing, using MC and size 5 (3.75 mm) shorter circular or double pointed needles, place the 2 stitches from the safety pin at underarm onto the needle, pick up and knit 3 stitches for every CC and 3 sts for every MC stripe (1 stitch in each ridge).

When you reach the 2 sts at the beginning of the round, K1, place marker for the center of underarm. Join in the rnd.

long sleeve

Knit 5 rounds.

Decrease Round: K2tog, knit to 2 sts before marker, SSK.

Repeat last 6 rnds until sleeve is 7 (9, 10, 11)" long or 1" less than desired length. Do not decrease to less than 38 (40, 42, 44) sts. Try it on the recipient for length.

cuff

Change to size 3 (3.25 mm) double pointed needles.

Rnd 1: Purl, decreasing to 38 (40, 42, 44) sts, if necessary.

Rnd 2: Knit.

Rnd 3: Purl.

Repeat last 2 rnds 3 (3, 4, 4) times — 5 (5, 6, 6) Garter Stitch ridges showing on RS.

Bind off knitwise.

finishing

Weave in any loose ends.

Buttons

Set a shank button over the buttonhole on the appropriate side (left band for girls and right band for boys). Using button twist thread, close the hole as you attach the button. After 2–3 passes of the thread, attach a small shirt button on the WS of the band and sew through both buttons. This adds strength and stability to the button.

sassy stripes
hoodie vest

• •

This hoodie vest is a great addition to any child's wardrobe and is a popular choice for the kids today. It's easy to knit with minimal shaping and maximum style. Knit it in the stripes, as shown, or in many colors.

Style Notes: Knit in one piece, from the bottom up. Work the body of the vest, including the button bands, back and forth in one piece to the armholes. Then divide for the 2 Fronts and the Back which are worked separately, also back and forth. After joining the shoulders, knit the hood to the top. To finish armholes, pick up the stitches at the edge and knit in the round. I suggest weaving in ends as you go, so to finish just sew on buttons and your hoodie is ready for that special child to wear.

Designer: Dana Gibbons
Experience Level: Enthusiastic Beginner

sizes
To fit Child: 1 (2, 4, 6) years

finished measurements
Chest: 24 (26, 28, 30)"
Body Length: 12 (14, 14, 16)"
Sleeve Length: 6½ (8, 10, 12)"

materials
DK, Light Worsted Weight Yarn(1.75 ounces/
    133 yards, 50 grams/123 meters per ball):
        Blue (MC) 3 (3, 4, 4) balls
        Green (CC) 2 (2, 3, 3) balls
Size 5 (3.75 mm) 24" (60 cm) circular needle OR
    pair of straight needles
Size 3 (3.25 mm) 24" (60 cm) circular needle OR
    pair of straight needles

Set of size 3 (3.25 mm) double pointed needles

5 (6, 7, 8) ½-inch shank buttons

5 (6, 7, 8) small shirt buttons

Buttonhole twist craft thread (color for sewing
    on buttons)

2 markers

2 small safety pins or stitch holders

3 larger stitch holders or spare needles for holding
    non-working stitches

gauge

22 sts = 4" (10 cm) on size 5 (3.75 mm) in Garter
Stitch or size needed to obtain gauge

10 rows in Garter Rib Pattern = 1"

garter stitch rib pattern

Row 1: With CC knit.

Row 2: With CC purl.

Rows 3 and 4: Repeat Rows 1 and 2.

Rows 5–10: With MC, knit (makes 3 ridges on RS).
Repeat 10 rows.

let's begin

NOTE: Place buttonholes on both the right and left
button bands. The buttons and buttonholes will line
up perfectly when you sew the buttons over the holes
on the appropriate button band.

With size 3 (3.25 mm) 24" (60 cm) circular or straight
needles and MC, cast on 136 (152, 164,176) sts.
Working back and forth:
Starting on the WS, knit 9 (9, 11, 11) rows — 5 (5, 6,
6) Garter Stitch ridges showing on RS with cast on
row counted as first ridge.

NOTE: Do not cut the MC but carry it up the sides
loosely as you work.

Row 1: (RS) With larger circular or straight needles
and CC, K5, place marker, knit to last 5 sts, place
marker, K5.

Row 2: K5, slip marker, purl to next marker, slip
marker, K5.

Row 3 (Buttonholes): (RS) Continuing with CC, K1,

K2tog, YO, K2, slip marker, knit to next marker, slip marker, K2, YO, K2tog, K1.

Row 4: K5, purl to last 5 sts, K5. (Buttonhole sits between 2 Garter Stitch ridges.)

Rows 5–10: With MC, knit every row, do not cut MC — makes 3 ridges on RS.

Row 11: (RS) With CC, knit.

Row 12: K5, purl to last 5 sts, K5.

Row 13: Knit.

Row 14: K5, purl to last 5 sts, K5.

Rows 15–20: With MC, knit every row.

Work the 10 rows of the Garter Stitch Rib Pattern, maintaining the button bands at the Front edges in Garter Stitch as set and **at the same time** placing buttonholes in every second CC band as above. Work until you have 6 (7, 7, 8) CC bands, ending with Row 10 (MC).

Divide for Right Front

Row 1: (RS) With CC, K35 (40, 43, 46) sts, turn. Leave remaining stitches on a spare needle or stitch holder.

Row 2: Purl to last 5 sts, K5.

Row 3: Knit, (placing buttonhole if necessary).

Row 4: Purl to last 5 sts, K5.

Continue working Garter Stitch Rib Pattern as set, maintaining button band on Right Front edge, placing buttonholes every second CC band as established until 5 (6, 6, 7) more CC stripes have been worked, ending with Row 4 (stripe with buttonhole).

Decrease for neck edge: Do not make any more buttonholes.

Next Row: (RS) With MC, K5, slip marker, K1, SSK, knit to end of row.

Next Row: (WS) Knit.

Repeat last 2 rows twice more — 32 (37, 40, 43) sts.

Next Row: With CC, K5, slip marker, K1, SSK, knit to end of row.

Next Row: Purl to last 5 sts, slip marker, K5.

Repeat last 2 rows once more — 30 (35, 38, 41) sts.

With MC, knit 6 rows.

Place these sts on a stitch holder or spare needle.

Divide for Back

Return to stitches placed on first holder.

With RS facing, put first 2 sts from holder onto a safety pin for armhole, reattach CC, K62 (68, 74, 80) sts from holder, turn. Leave rest of sts on holder for Left Front.

Next Row: Purl.

Next Row: Knit.

Next Row: Purl.

Continue to work Garter Stitch Rib Pattern until Back measures the same as the Right Front.

Joining Right Front to right shoulder of Back:

Slip stitches of Right Front onto a larger double pointed needle. With WS facing, start at armhole edge, work 3-Needle Bind Off on RS of work, binding off 18 (20, 22, 24) sts. Break yarn and pull through stitch on right needle. Note: Leave all the remaining stitches on both of the needles on hold for hood, keep the marker in place.

Return to body of vest to finish Left Front.

Left Front

With RS facing, put first 2 sts on safety pin for armhole, reattach CC, knit to end of row, turn.

Next Row: K5, slip marker, purl to end of row.

Continue Garter Stitch Rib Pattern, maintaining button band and continue to place buttonholes as

set. Work until 5 (6, 6, 7) more CC stripes have been worked, ending with Row 4 (CC stripe with buttonhole).

Decrease for neck edge: Do not make any more buttonholes.

Next Row: (RS) With MC, knit to last 8 sts, K2tog, K1, slip marker, K5.

Next Row: Knit.

Repeat last 2 rows twice more — 32 (37, 40, 43) sts.

Next Row: With CC, knit to last 8 sts, K2tog, K1, slip marker, K5.

Next Row: K5, purl to end.

Repeat last 2 rows once more — 30 (35, 38, 41) sts. With MC, knit 6 rows.

Joining Left Front to left shoulder of Back:

With WS of Left Front and left shoulder of Back facing, starting at armhole edge, work 3-Needle Bind Off on RS, binding off 18 (20, 22, 24) sts. Break yarn and pull through stitch on right needle. Note: Leave all the remaining stitches on both of the needles on hold for hood; keep the marker in place.

You are now going to continue knitting these stitches for the hood.

hood

On RS with size 5 (3.75 mm) circular needle and CC in sequence, starting at Right Front K11 (14, 15, 16) sts from Right Front, pick up and K2 sts from shoulder join to close the gap. K24 (26, 28, 30) sts from back of neck, pick up and K2 sts to close gap at left shoulder, K11 (14, 15, 16) sts from Left Front, turn — 50 (58, 62, 66) sts.

Next Row (WS): K5, slip marker, purl to next marker, slip marker, K5.

Next Row: K6, *M1, K2; repeat from * to last 4 sts,

slip marker K4 — 70 (82, 88, 94) sts.

Next Row: K5, slip marker, purl to last 5 sts, slip marker, K5.

Continue even in Garter Stitch Rib Pattern as set, maintaining Garter Stitch button bands at each end (do not make buttonholes), until hood measures 7 (7½, 8, 9)" or desired length from Increase Row, ending with Row 4 or Row 10 of Garter Stitch Rib Pattern.

Place half of stitches on the smaller circular needle. Working from Front of hood, with WS facing, work 3-Needle Bind Off on all sts.

Vest armhole edging

Worked in the round. With RS of work facing, using MC and size 3 (3¼ mm) shorter circular or double pointed needles, place the 2 sts from the safety pin onto the needle, pick up and knit 3 sts for every CC stripe and 3 sts for every MC stripe (1 stitch in each ridge). When you reach the 2 sts at the beginning of the row, K1, place marker at center underarm.

Join in the round.

Purl 1 rnd.

Knit 1 rnd.

Repeat last 2 rounds once.

Bind off purlwise.

finishing

Weave in any loose ends.

Buttons

Set a shank button over the buttonhole on the appropriate side (left band for girls and right band for boys). Using button twist thread, close the hole as you attach the button. After 2–3 passes of the thread, attach a small shirt button on the WS of the band and sew through both buttons. This adds strength and stability to the button.

la petite **chanel**

· ·

The 100th birthday of Coco Chanel marked the resurgence of her most popular and recognizable signature pieces. Women and now children alike can enjoy the tailored and fashionable appeal of the Chanel Jacket, knit to perfection with an easy slip stitch pattern.

Style Notes: Knit in one piece from the bottom up. Ring markers separate the fronts and back, making the construction easy and flowing. Pick up and knit the sleeves from the shoulders down to the wrists. Sewing is required for the lapel edging and pockets.

Add the easy Garter Slip Stitch Pattern and create a wonderful textured fabric. By changing the finishes or moving the buttons you could personalize the appearance of this classic jacket.

Designer: Karen Lawrence
Experience Level: Intermediate

sizes
To fit Child: 1 (2, 4, 6) years

finished measurements
Chest: 24 (26, 28, 30)"
Body Length: 11 (12, 14, 16)"
Sleeve Length: 6½ (8, 10, 12)"

materials
DK, Light Worsted Weight Yarn (4 ounces/
    250 yards, 125 grams/230 meters per skein):
        Dark Pink (A) 1 (1, 1½, 1½) skein
        Pale Pink (B) 1 (1, 1½, 1½) skein
        Cream (C) 1 (1, 1½, 1½) skein
DK, Light Worsted Weight Eyelash Yarn (1.75 ounces/
    152 yards, 50 grams/140 meters per ball):
        Beige 1 (1, 1, 2) ball eyelash for trim

Two ½-inch gold shank buttons

Ring markers

Stitch holders

Size 5 (3.75 mm) 24" (60 cm) circular needle

Size 6 (4.0 mm) 16" (40 cm) circular needle

Size 6 (4.0 mm) 24" (60 cm) circular needle

Set of 6 (4.0 mm) double pointed needles size
    for sleeves

gauge

Sweater: 28 sts = 4" (10 cm) on size 6 (4.0 mm) over Garter Slip Stitch Pattern or size needed to obtain gauge

Garter Slip Stitch Pattern:

Row 1: (RS) With A, K2, *SL1(p), K2, repeat from * to end of row.

Row 2: With A, knit.

Row 3: With B, K2 *SL1(p), K2, repeat from * to end of row.

Row 4: With B, knit.

Row 5: With C, K2, *SL1(p), K2, repeat from * to end of row.

Row 6: With C Knit.

Repeat these 6 rows.

NOTE: I used cotton and it tends not to have much elasticity. I found that if I held the yarn firmly as I knit, the consistency of the fabric was wonderful.

let's begin

With smaller circular needle, and eyelash yarn, cast on 169 (182, 197, 209) sts.

Set Up Row: K42 (45, 49, 52), place marker, K85 (92, 99,105), place marker, K42 (45, 49, 52).

With eyelash yarn, knit every row until piece measures 1" from beginning. Break yarn.

Change to A and larger 24"(60 cm) circular needle, work in the Garter Slip Stitch Pattern until garment measures 5 (5, 6½, 8)" from cast on edge, ending after a knit row (WS).

right front

Next Row: Work to first marker in pattern, turn, leave remaining stitches on circular needle.

Next Row: Bind off 5 (8, 6, 9) sts for underarm, and knit to the end of the row — 37 (37, 43, 43) sts. Work only Right Front stitches until garment measures 9 (10, 11½, 13½)" from cast on edge, ending after a knit row (WS).

Neck Shaping

Continuing in color and pattern stitch as set, with RS facing, bind off 7 (7, 10, 10) sts at the beginning of the next row, work in pattern to end of row. Continue in pattern as set, decreasing 1 stitch at the beginning of every alternate row at neck edge 7 (7, 9, 9) times — 23 (23, 24, 24) sts.

Continue even in pattern stitch until Right Front measures 11 (12, 14, 16)" from the cast on edge. Leave these stitches on a stitch holder.

back

With RS facing, at underarm attach appropriate color to continue the pattern, bind off 5 (8, 6, 9) sts and knit in pattern to the next marker, turn.

Next Row: Bind off 5 (8, 6, 9) sts for underarm and knit in pattern as set to the end of the row — 75 (76, 87, 87) sts.

Work even in pattern, with no further shaping until Back measures 11 (12, 14, 16)" from cast on edge (matches the total length of Right Front).

Leave remaining 75 (76, 87, 87) sts on a stitch holder.

left front

With RS facing, at underarm attach appropriate color to continue in pattern as set for Left Front, bind off 5 (8, 6, 9) sts at the armhole edge of the work, work in pattern to end of row — 37 (37, 43, 43) sts.

Work even in pattern stitch until work from beginning measures 9 (10, 11½, 13½)", ending after a RS row.

Neck Shaping

Next Row: (WS) Bind off 7 (7, 10, 10) sts at neck edge, work in pattern to end of row — 30 (30, 33, 33). Continue in pattern as set, decrease 1 stitch on every alternate row at the neck edge 7 (7, 9, 9) times — 23 (23, 24, 24) sts.

Continue even in pattern stitch until Left Front measures 11 (12, 14, 16)" from the cast on edge. Leave these stitches on a stitch holder.

join the shoulders

Turn garment inside out, and using a 3-Needle Bind Off technique, bind off the 23 (23, 24, 24) Left Front and Left Back stitches together and the 23 (23, 24, 24) Right Front and Right Back stitches together. Leave remaining 29 (30, 39, 39) sts at back of neck on a holder for later.

sleeves (make two)

NOTE: Double pointed needles are recommended for the sleeves but a 16" (40 cm) circular can be used for the first few rows, if preferred. At some point though as the sleeves decrease in circumference, double points will become necessary. I found the double points enabled a much more consistent fabric.

At the center point of the underarm, with B and size 6 (4.0 mm) double pointed needle, pick up and knit 83

(98, 104, 110) sts around armhole, place marker to mark the beginning of each round.

With B, purl 1 round.

Work 6 rounds of Garter Slip Stitch Pattern below.

Garter Slip Stitch Pattern – worked in the rnd for sleeve:

NOTE: Because the sleeves are worked in the round, all previous knit rows in the Garter Slip Stitch Pattern will now be worked as purl rnds.

Rnd 1: With C, K2, *SL1(p), K2; repeat from * to end of rnd.

Rnd 2: With C, purl.

Rnd 3: With A, K2, *SL1(p), K2; repeat from * to end of rnd.

Rnd 4: With A, purl.

Rnd 5: With B, K2, *SL1(p), K2; repeat from * to end of rnd.

Rnd 6: With B, purl.

Decrease Rnd: K2tog, work in pattern to last 2 sts, SSK.

Continue to work in Garter Slip Stitch Pattern adjusting for decreases. Work Decrease Rnd on next and every following 4th (4th, 6th, 6th) rnd, 19 (24, 21, 21) times, then work Decrease Rnd every 2nd (2nd, 4th, 4th) rnd until sleeve measures 5½ (7, 9, 11)" from underarm or desired length before cuff. Do not decrease to less than 43 (44, 52, 52) sts. If necessary, work even in pattern to reach desired length.

NOTE: The slip stitches in the Garter Slip Stitch Pattern make the vertical ridges seen in the sleeve.

You can use these slip stitch ridges to realign the beginning of your pattern as you work the decreases down the sleeve.

trim

Cuff

With eyelash yarn, purl around, decreasing if necessary to 43 (44, 52, 52) sts.

Work 1" in Garter Stitch (knit 1 rnd, purl 1 rnd) — 43 (44, 52, 52) sts.

Bind off loosely.

Front Edges

With eyelash yarn and size 5 (3.75 mm) needle, with RS facing, pick up and knit 1 stitch for each Garter Stitch ridge along Right Front of jacket.

Knit 5 rows and bind off.

Fold the eyelash trim over to WS of the jacket and sew into place, covering the cotton edge of the garment.

Repeat for Left Front.

Neckband

With eyelash yarn and size 5 (3.75 mm) circular needle, with RS facing, pick up and K7 (7, 10, 10) sts along front neck, and 9 (9, 11, 11) sts evenly along neck shaping. Pick up and knit 1 stitch for each Garter Stitch ridge to top of shoulder, knit the 29 (30, 39, 39) back of neck stitches from holder and then pick up and knit 1 stitch for each Garter Stitch ridge down left side of neck. Pick up and knit 9 (9, 11, 11) sts evenly along neck shaping and 7 (7, 10, 10) sts along neck. Knit 6 rows loosely and bind off.

Front Faux Pockets

Measure 1½" in from Front edge and 1½" down from beginning of neck shaping, and mark (with a safety pin) where these 2 measurements intersect. Beginning at the mark, with eyelash yarn, pick up and knit 16 sts in a straight line across the Right Front.
Knit 3 rows and bind off loosely.
With the ends created, tack the eyelash flap in place downward, so that the flap lays over a few rows of the Garter Slip Stitch Pattern, creating faux pocket top. Adorn with a button, if desired. Work Left Front faux pocket top to correspond.

finishing

Sew buttons to flaps of faux pockets. Sew in all ends.

little boy blue
striped vest

Here is a simple, easy vest. You can knit this vest in one color or use up bits of yarn to create a multicolored design. The classic pattern will never go out of style.

Style Notes: Knit in one piece, back and forth on circular needles. Make buttonholes on both sides of the border so the buttons are perfectly aligned when you close up the hole when sewing on the buttons. (This also makes it possible to choose whether it's for a boy or a girl when the knitting is complete and you're ready to sew on the buttons).

Designer: Lynda Gemmell
Experience Level: Enthusiastic Beginner

sizes
To fit Child: 1 (2, 4, 6) years

finished measurements
Chest: 24 (26, 28, 30)"
Length: 11 (12, 13, 14)"

materials
Worsted Weight Yarn (1.75 ounces/84 yards,
    50 grams/77 meters per balls):
        Navy MC 3 (3, 4, 4) balls
        Blue (A) 1 (1, 1, 1) balls
        Purple (B) 1 (1, 1, 1)
Size 8 (5.0 mm) 24" (60 cm) circular needle
Size 8 (5.0 mm) needle (one extra needle to work
    3–Needle Bind Off)
Size 6 (4.0 mm) 24" (60 cm) circular needle
Stitch holder
3 (4, 4, 5) ½-inch buttons

gauge

18 sts = 4" (10 cm) on size 8 (5.0 mm) needle or size needed to obtain gauge

Begin with striped border

With MC and size 6 (4.0 mm) needle, cast on 108 (116, 128, 136) sts.

Work back and forth on circular needle:

Knit 6 rows (3 ridges showing on RS). Break yarn.

With A, knit 2 rows (1 ridge).

With B, knit 2 rows, break yarn (1 ridge).

With A, knit 2 rows, break yarn (1 ridge).

body

Row 1: (RS) With MC, knit.

Row 2: Knit.

Row 3 (Buttonhole): K2, bind off 2 sts, knit to last 4 sts, bind off 2 sts (1 stitch will be on the right needle), K1.

Row 4 (Buttonhole): K2, cast on 2 sts, knit to last 2 sts, cast on 2 sts, K2.

Rows 5 and 6: Knit.

Rows 7 and 8: With A, knit (1 ridge).

Rows 9 and 10: With B, knit. Break yarn (1 ridge).

Rows 11 and 12: With A, knit. Break yarn (1 ridge).

Repeat last 12 rows (or 6 ridges), 2 (3, 3, 4) more times — 3 (4, 4, 5) buttonholes.

V-Neck Shaping

Change to larger needle and MC.

Next Row: (RS) Knit.

Next Row: K6, purl to last 6 sts, K6.

Repeat last 2 rows 2 (0, 2, 0) times more.

Next Row: (RS) K6, SSK, knit to last 8 sts, K2tog, K6 — 106 (114, 126, 134) sts.

Armhole

Work Garter Stitch border underneath the armhole first.

Row 1: With RS facing, K6, P12 (14, 17, 19), K16 (armhole border), P38 (42, 48, 52), K16 (armhole border), P12 (14, 17, 19), K6.

Row 2: (RS) Knit.

Row 3: Repeat Row 1.

Row 4: K6, SSK, knit to last 8 sts, K2tog, K6 — 104 (112, 124, 132) sts.

Row 5: K6, P11 (13, 16, 18), K6, bind off 4 sts, (1 stitch on right needle after the gap), K5, P38 (42, 48, 52), K6, bind off 4 sts, (1 stitch on right needle after gap), K5, P11 (13, 16, 18), K6.

NOTE: Front has 23 (25, 28, 30) sts, gap, Back has 50 (54, 60, 64) sts, gap, Front has 23 (25, 28, 30) sts.

right front

Work the Right Front of the vest first. If you wish, you can put the Back and Left Front sts on stitch holders or spare yarn while you work the Right Front.

Row 1: With RS facing, K23 (25, 28, 30) sts of Front.

Row 2: K6, purl to last 6 sts, K6.

Row 3: K6, SSK, knit to end of row.

Row 4: K6, purl to last 6 sts, K6.

Row 5: Knit.

Row 6: K6, purl to last 6 sts, K6.

Repeat Rows 1–6 until 20 (22, 24, 26) sts remain. Then repeat Rows 1–4 only until 14 (16, 18, 20) sts remain.

Work in pattern as set without any more decreases until the piece measures 11 (12, 13, 14)" from cast on edge, ending with a WS row. Break yarn. Place these stitches onto a stitch holder, double pointed needle, or piece of spare yarn.

NOTE: If you have put the stitches onto a double pointed needle, wind an elastic band around each of the ends of the needle to keep the stitches from slipping off.

back

Row 1: With RS facing, reattach yarn and K50 (54, 60, 64) sts of Back.

Row 2: K6, purl to last 6 sts, K6.

Row 3: K6, SSK, knit to last 8 sts, K2tog, K6.

Row 4: K6, purl to last 6 sts, K6.

Row 5: Knit.

Row 6: K6, purl to last 6 sts, K6.

Repeat last 6 rows 1 more time — 46 (50, 56, 60) sts.

Work even in pattern as set with no further decreases until Back is 3 ridges short of the Front (count the ridges on the underarm border).

Back Border

Row 1: Knit.

Row 2: K6, P2 (4, 6, 8), knit to last 8 (10, 12, 14) sts,

P2 (4, 6, 8), K6.

Row 3: K8 (10, 12, 14), K2tog, knit to last 10 (12, 14, 16) sts, K2tog, K8 (10, 12, 14).

Repeat Rows 2 and 3 once more.

Work Row 2 once more (3 ridges now showing on RS at center of back of neck). Break yarn. Put these stitches on a stitch holder or piece of yarn.

left front

Row 1: With RS facing, reattach yarn and K23 (25, 28, 30) sts of Front.

Row 2: K6, purl to last 6 sts, K6.

Row 3: Knit to last 8 sts, K2tog, K6.

Row 4: K6, purl to last 6 sts, K6.

Row 5: Knit.

Row 6: K6, purl to last 6 sts, K6.

Repeat Rows 1–6 until 20 (22, 24, 26) sts remain. Then repeat Rows 1–4 **only** until 14 (16, 18, 20) sts remain.

Work even in pattern as set until the piece measures 11 (12, 13, 14)" from cast on edge, ending with a WS row. Do not break the yarn.

Joining the Shoulders

You are now going to join the shoulders and bind off the back of neck stitches. Slip the Back stitches onto the other end of the circular needle. Fold over Left Front to Back with RS together. Beginning at the armhole edge using a third needle of a similar size and the 3-Needle Bind Off technique, bind off the Left Front and Back. Bind off the back of neck stitches to the last 14 (16, 18, 20) sts, then using the 3-Needle Bind Off technique again with RS together, bind off the Right Front and Back.

finishing

Sew on buttons and sew in ends.

northern lights
sweater and hat

This sweater is inspired by classic Nordic designs, making it a timeless favorite that can be passed from one child to another. It is an appreciated hand-me-down. The matching ski hat completes the outfit, however, do not hesitate to just knit this little treasure all on its own. It is a great way to use up leftover yarn.

Style Notes: Knit in the round from bottom up. Pick up and knit sleeves from the shoulders to the wrist.

Designer: Megan Lacey
Experience Level: Intermediate

sizes
To fit Child: 1 (2, 4, 6) years
Hat: 1-2 (4, 6) years
Chest Measurement: 20 (22, 24, 26)"

finished measurements
Sweater:
Chest: 24 (26, 28, 30)"
Body Length: 12 (13, 15, 17)"
Armhole Depth: 6 (7, 7½, 8)"
Sleeve Length: 6½ (8, 10, 12)"
Hat:
Hat Circumference: 17 (18, 19)"

materials
Worsted Weight Yarn (3.5 ounces/220 yards,
    100 grams/203 meters per ball):
    Sweater:
        Red (A) 2 balls
        Navy (B) 2 balls
        Lime Green (C) 1 ball
        Orange (D) 1 ball
    Hat:
        Red (A) 1 balls
        Navy (B) 1 balls

Lime Green (C) small amount of leftover yarn
Orange (D) small amount of leftover yarn
1 clasp
2 markers
Set of size 6 (4.0 mm) double pointed needles
Size 7 (4.5 mm) 16" (60 cm) circular needle
Size 6 (4.0 mm) 24" (60 cm) circular needle
Set of size 7 (4.5 mm) double pointed needles

gauge

20 sts = 4" (10 cm) on size 7 (4.5 mm) needle over
Stockinette Stitch or size needed to obtain gauge

body

With A and size 6 (4.0 mm) circular needle, cast on 60
(66, 69, 75) sts, place marker, cast on another 60 (66,
69, 75) sts, place marker — 120 (132, 138, 150) sts
on needle.
Join in the round, being careful not to twist stitches.
Rnd 1: Work [K1, P1] rib to end of round.
Continue to work rib as established for 1 (1, 1½, 1½)"
from cast on edge.
Change to size 7 (4.5 mm) circular needle and work
Chart A (see page 95) for approximately 3 (3, 4, 5½)"

ending on Row 2 or 7 of Chart (sweater measures 4
(4, 5½, 7)" from cast on edge).
Work Chart B.

Divide for armholes: Break A and attach B, knit first
60 (66, 69, 75) sts for Front. Place remaining stitches
for the Back on a stitch holder.

work front first

With B work in Stockinette Stitch for 2 (2, 2, 2½)"
ending after a WS row.
Divide for Front opening: With RS facing, knit across
28 (31, 32, 35) sts, turn.

Left Front

Continue to work Left Front in Stockinette Stitch for a
further 2 (2½, 3, 3)", ending after a RS row.

Neck Shaping

With WS facing, at neck edge, bind off first 4 (5, 6, 6)
sts, purl to end of row.
Knit 1 row.
At neck edge, bind off 2 sts at the beginning of next
row, purl to end.

Knit 1 row.

Decrease 1 stitch at the beginning of the next row and every alternate row 1 (1, 0, 1) time more. There should now be 20 (22, 23, 25) sts remaining.

Continue to work even on these stitches until armhole measures 5 (6, 6 ½, 7)" and ending after a WS row. Break B.

With C, knit 1 row.

With A, purl 1 row.

With D, knit 1 row.

With A, purl 1 row.

With A, knit 1 row. Place these shoulder stitches on waste yarn or spare needle.

Right Front:

At Front opening, attach B to remaining 32 (35, 37, 40) sts and with RS facing,

Bind off first 4 (4, 5, 5) sts for neck opening, knit to end of row.

Work back and forth in Stockinette Stitch for 2 (2 ½, 3, 3)" ending after a WS row.

Neck Shaping

With RS facing, at neck edge bind off first 4 (5, 6, 6) sts, knit to end of row.

Purl 1 row.

At neck edge, bind off 2 sts at the beginning of next row, knit to end of row.

Purl 1 row.

Decrease 1 stitch at the beginning of the next row and every alternate row 1 (1, 0, 1) time more. There should now be 20 (22, 23, 25) sts remaining.

Continue to work even on these stitches until armhole measures 5 (6, 6 ½, 7)" ending after a WS row. Break B.

With C, knit 1 row.

With A, purl 1 row.

With D, knit 1 row.

With A, purl 1 row.

With A, knit 1 row. Place these shoulder stitches on waste yarn or spare needle.

back

Join B to remaining 60 (66, 69, 75) sts and work back and forth in Stockinette Stitch until armhole measures 5 (6, 6½, 7)" ending after a WS row.

Work first shoulder:

Knit across 22 (24, 25, 27) sts, place next 16 (18, 19, 21) sts onto a stitch holder for back of neck, turn. Break B.

With WS facing, join C, decrease 1 stitch at the beginning of row, purl to end.

With A, knit 1 row.

With D, decrease 1 stitch at the beginning of row and purl to end of row.

With A, knit 1 row.

With A, purl 1 row. Place 20 (22, 23, 25) shoulder sts on waste yarn or spare needle.

Second Shoulder

With RS facing, at neck edge on opposite side of back of neck sts, join B to 22 (24, 25, 27) sts of second shoulder and decrease 1 stitch at beginning of row, knit to end of row.

With C, purl 1 row.

With A, decrease 1 stitch at the beginning of row and knit to end of row.

With D, purl 1 row.

With A, knit 1 row.

With A, purl 1 row. Place the remaining 20 (22, 23, 25) shoulder sts on waste yarn or spare needle.

Join shoulders: using 3-Needle Bind Off, join Front and Back shoulder stitches together with RS facing.

sleeves

With size 7 (4.5 mm) 16" (40 cm) circular needle (change to double pointed needles when needed) and C, beginning at underarm, pick up and knit 60 (66, 78, 84) sts evenly around armhole. Join in the round and place a marker between the first and last stitch. Work Chart C.

Work Chart A, starting on Row 5 or Row 10 to match Front, **at the same time** work the Sleeve Decrease Round every 3rd round until sleeves measure 5½ (7, 8½ , 10½)" or desired length before cuff (do not decrease to less than 38 (38, 44, 44 sts).

Sleeve Decrease Round: K1, SL1, K1, psso, knit in pattern to last 3 stitches, K2tog, K1.

cuff

Change to size 6 (4.0 mm) double pointed needles and with A, knit 1 round, decreasing if necessary to 38 (38, 44, 44) sts.

Work [K1, P1] rib for 1 (1, 1½ , 1½)" and bind off in rib.

Work second sleeve in the same manner.

neckline

With size 6 (4.0 mm) 16" (40 cm) circular needle and A, start at the bottom corner of Right Front opening and pick up and knit 20 (20, 23, 23) sts up RS of opening. Pick up and K14 (16, 18, 18) sts around Right Side of neck, pick up and K6 sts down right back of neck, K16 (18, 19, 21) stitches from back of neck stitch holder. Pick up and knit 6 sts up left back of neck, 14 (16, 18, 18) sts around left side neckline and 20 (20, 23, 23) sts down left side of opening — 96 (102, 113, 115) sts.

Turn and knit all stitches. Break A.

With B and with RS facing, bind off 20 (20, 23, 23) sts up the side of neck opening only, knit around 56 (62, 67, 69) neck sts, bind off 20 (20, 23, 23) sts down side of neck opening.

Reattach B and work [K1,P1] rib on remaining neckband stitches for 3". Bind off in rib.

finishing

Sew sides of neck opening to bind off edge at bottom of Front opening. Fold collar in half and sew to inside of sweater. Whipstitch sides of collar closed. Sew in all ends. Sew clasp just below collar to close opening. Block with damp cloth.

hat

With B and size 7 (4.5 mm) circular needle, cast on 84 (90, 96) sts. Place marker and join in the rnd, being careful not to twist stitches.

Inner lining of hat: Knit 10 (12, 12) rounds.

Fold Rnd: Purl 1 rnd.

Work Chart D.

Next Rnd: With A, knit.

Work Chart A.

Continue to repeat Chart A until hat measures 6 (6 ½, 7)" from purl Fold Rnd.

Shape Crown

Decrease Rnd: With A, *K1, K2tog; repeat from * to end of rnd — 56 (60, 64) sts.

Next and every alternate rnd: Knit.

Decrease Rnd: *K2tog; repeat from * to end of rnd — 28 (30, 32) sts.

Decrease Rnd: *K2tog; repeat from * to end of rnd — 14 (15, 16) sts.

For Sizes 2 and 6 ONLY:

Decrease Rnd: *K2tog; repeat from * to end of rnd — 7 (8) sts.

For Size 4 ONLY: *K2tog; repeat from * to the last st, K1 — 8 sts.

finishing

Break yarn, thread yarn through remaining 7 (8, 8) sts, pull opening closed, take yarn to WS and fasten end of yarn. Make large pompom, using all colors and sew to top of hat. Fold cast-on edge to the inside of hat along the fold line and tack down. Block with damp cloth.

Legend

☐ Red (A)
● Navy (B)
◗ Lime (C)
+ Orange (D)

NOTE: When knitting from Chart A, B, C and D, always read rows right to left when working in the rnd.

Chart A

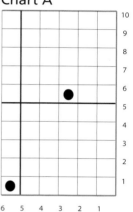

Chart B

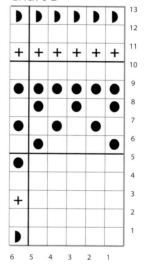

Chart C

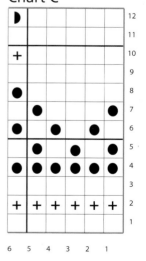

Chart D (Hat)

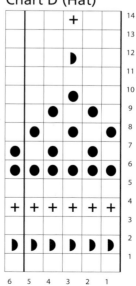

pretty in points **vest**

Vests can be fun for a first full garment. They are small and fast, and you do not have to knit the sleeves! You start this vest by knitting all the little Garter Stitch points first. You could also knit the Garter Stitch points and borders in one color and the body in another.

Style Notes: Knit in one piece, back and forth on circular needles. No sewing required.

Designer: Lynda Gemmell
Experience Level: Enthusiastic Beginner

sizes
To fit Child: 1 (2, 4, 6) years

finished measurements
Chest: 24 (26, 28, 30)"
Length: 10 (11, 12, 13)"

materials
Heavy Worsted Weight Yarn (1.75 ounces/84 yards,
    50 grams/77 meters ball):
        Blue 3 (3, 4, 4) balls
Size 8 (5.0 mm) 24"(60 cm) circular needle
Size 8 (5.0 mm) extra needle to work
    3-Needle Bind Off
Size 6 (4.0 mm) 24"(60 cm) circular needle
Seven ½-inch buttons

gauge
18 sts = 4" (10 cm) with size 8 (5.0 mm) needle or size needed to obtain gauge

begin border with the points
With size 6 (4.0 mm) needle, cast on 2 sts.
Work back and forth on circular needle:
Next Row: Knit 2 sts.

Next Row: K1, M1, knit to end of row.
Repeat the last row until you have 12 stitches on the needle. Break yarn. Leave finished point on needle. Make 8 (8, 9, 10) more points — 9 (9, 10, 11) points in total.

Join up all the points by knitting across all the stitches of the points on the needle — 108 (108, 120, 132) sts. Knit every row until piece measures 3" from tips of points.

Change to larger circular needle.
Increase Row: (RS) Knit, increasing 0 (8, 8, 4) sts evenly across row — 108 (116, 128, 136) sts.
Row 1: K5, purl to last 5 sts, K5.
Row 2: Knit.
Row 3 (Buttonhole): (WS) K5, purl to last 5 sts, K2, bind off 1 stitch, (1 stitch on right needle after bind off), K1.
Row 4 (Buttonhole): (RS) K2, cast on 1 stitch, knit to end of row.
Repeat the last 4 rows until the vest measures approximately 5 (5½, 6, 7)", or desired length, from the points,

ending with a Row 4 (work a little longer if needed, to finish with Row 4).

Armhole

You will begin by working the armhole border first.
Row 1: With WS facing, K5, P15 (17, 20, 22), K14 (armhole border), P40 (44, 50, 54), K14 (armhole border), P15 (17, 20, 22), K5 — 108 (108, 120, 132) sts.
Row 2: Knit.
Row 3 (Buttonhole): (WS) K5, P15 (17, 20, 22), K14 (armhole border), P40 (44, 50, 54), K14 (armhole border), purl to last 5 sts, K2, bind off 1 stitch, (1 stitch on right needle after bind off), K1.
Row 4 (Buttonhole): K2, cast on 1 stitch, knit to end.
Next Row: K5, P15 (17, 20, 22), K5, bind off 4 sts, (1 stitch on right needle after the gap), K4, P40 (44, 50, 54), K5, bind off 4 sts, (1 stitch on right needle after the gap), K4, purl to last 5 sts, K5.

NOTE: Front has 25 (27, 30, 32) sts, armhole gap, Back has 50 (54, 60, 64) sts, armhole gap, Front has 25 (27, 30, 32) sts.

right front

You will now be working on the Right Front of the vest. You may wish to put Back and Left Front sts onto a holder or spare yarn.

Row 1: (RS) K5, SSK, knit to end of row — 24 (26, 29, 31) sts.

Row 2: K5, purl to last 5 sts, K5.

Row 3: Knit.

Row 4: K5, purl to last 5 sts, K5.

Repeat last 4 rows one more time.

Repeat Rows 1 and 2, until 13 (14, 15, 16) sts remain. Work in pattern as set without any more decreases until the vest measures 11 (12, 13, 14)" from points, ending with a WS row. Break yarn. Put these stitches on a stitch holder, a double pointed needle, or a piece of yarn.

NOTE: If you have put the stitches onto a double-pointed needle, wind an elastic band around each of the ends of the needle to keep the stitches from slipping off.

back

With RS facing, reattach yarn at underarm.

Row 1: K50 (54, 60, 64) sts of Back.

Row 2: K5, purl to last 5 sts, K5.

Row 3: Knit.

Row 4: K5, purl to last 5 sts, K5.

Row 5: K5, SSK, knit to last 7 sts, K2tog, K5.

Row 6: K5, purl to last 5 sts, K5.

Repeat the last 4 (6, 6, 6) rows, 4 more times — 40 (44, 50, 54) sts.

Work in pattern until the Back is 3 ridges short of the Right Front, counting ridges on armhole border.

Next Row: K5, P3 (4, 5, 6), knit to last 8 (9, 10, 11) sts, P3 (4, 5, 6), K5.

Next Row: K8 (9, 10, 11), K2tog, knit to last 10 (11, 12, 13) sts, K2tog, knit to end of row.

Repeat last 2 rows until 3 ridges are showing on RS, ending after a WS row. Break yarn. Put these stitches on a stitch holder, a double pointed needle, or a piece of yarn. (See previous note.)

left front

With RS facing, reattach yarn at underarm.

Row 1: Knit to last 7 sts, K2tog, K5.

Row 2: K5, purl to last 5 sts, K5.

Row 3: Knit.

Row 4: K5, purl to last 5 sts, K5.

Repeat last 4 rows one more time.

Repeat Rows 1 and 2, until 13 (14, 15, 16) sts remain. Work in pattern as set without any more decreases until the vest measures 11 (12, 13, 14)" from points, ending with a WS row. Do not break the yarn.

Joining the Shoulders

You are now going to join the shoulders and bind off the back of neck stitches. Slip the Back stitches onto the other end of the circular needle. Fold over Left Front to Back with RS together, and beginning at the armhole edge using a third needle of a similar size and the 3-Needle Bind Off technique, bind off the Left Front and Back. Bind off the back of neck stitches to the last 13 (14, 15, 16) sts, then using the 3-Needle Bind Off technique again with RS together, bind off the Right Front and Back.

finishing

Sew on buttons, sew in ends, and you are done!

pop **top**

This bare midriff slipover is just what the big girls are wearing! Knit in a simple texture stitch with a crisp cotton yarn, it is great for layering with a tee or wearing alone on a hot summer day. For a cozy vest, simply change the fiber and lengthen the body where indicated. There is detail in the shaping but the stitch pattern is simple. It creates neat, self-finishing edges, so when the last stitch is finished, you are too!

Style Notes: Knit from the bottom up in the round, with no sewing. Finish edges as you knit. The shaping is adventurous. The stitches are simple.

Designer: Shirl the Purl
Experience Level: Enthusiastic Beginner

sizes
To fit Child: 2 (4, 6, 8) years

finished measurements:
Chest: 24 (26, 28, 30)"
Length from Shoulder: 8 (8½, 9, 9½)"

materials
DK, Light Worsted Weight Yarn (4 ounces/250 yards, 125 grams/230 meters per skein):
    Green or Red 1 (1, 1, 1½) skein
Marker
Stitch holders and safety pins
Row counter (optional)
Size 6 (4.0 mm) 24" (60 cm) circular needle
Set of size 6 (4.0 mm) double pointed needles for 3-Needle Bind Off

gauge
22 sts = 4" (10 cm) in stitch pattern or size needed to obtain gauge

NOTE: There's magic in the self-finishing edges that

do not curl and need no additional trim. Here are some techniques that will keep your work neat.

Bind Off in Box Stitch Pattern

Work 2 stitches in pattern, pass first stitch over second stitch — 1 stitch bind off.
*Work next stitch in pattern, pass first stitch over this stitch — 2 stitch bind off.
Repeat from * until you bind off desired number of stitches. A loop will remain on right-hand needle. Continue in pattern, counting the loop as stitch number 1.

Decrease in Box Stitch Pattern

Decrease in pattern by working 2 stitches together, first determine, by looking at the row below, what the finished stitch should be: To make a knit stitch decrease K2tog and to make a purl stitch decrease P2tog.

Box Stitch Pattern

When working "in the round":
Rnds 1 and 2: Work [K2, P2] to end of round.
Rnds 3 and 4: Work [P2, K2] to end of round.
NOTE: When working back and forth on the Front

and Back of the garment, stitches can be reversed on the WS of the work. Learn to recognize the pattern visually. It is not hard!

let's begin

NOTE: When only one number is given, it applies to all sizes.

With circular needle, cast on 136 (144, 152, 160) sts. Join work in the round, taking care not to twist the stitches.
Work Rnd 1 of the Box Stitch Pattern, place marker at the end of round.
Work Rnds 2, 3, and 4 of Box Stitch Pattern.
Work Rnds 1–4 of Box Stitch 6 (7, 8, 9) more times.
For a longer top, repeat Rnds 1–4 until desired length to underarm, ending with Rnd 4.

Divide for Front and Back

Working in pattern, bind off 4 sts (see above "Bind Off in Box Stitch Pattern") for Right Armhole. Work in pattern as established for next 60 (64, 68, 72) sts for Back (including st remaining on right needle after bind off). Bind off in pattern next 8 sts for left armhole, work in pattern across Front to last 4 sts before end of rnd, bind off in pattern remaining 4 sts to complete right armhole. Break yarn. Place Front stitches on holder and mark RS of Back with a safety pin.

back

Work back and forth on the circular needle, working the first stitch of each row firmly.

Shape Armholes:

**With RS facing, join yarn at right armhole edge and decrease in pattern once (see page 102 "Decrease in Box Stitch Pattern") by working the first 2 sts of the row together firmly, work in pattern as established to last 2 sts, decrease once by working these 2 sts together in pattern — 58 (62, 66, 70) sts.

Next Row: Decrease in pattern once by working the first 2 sts of the row together firmly, work in pattern as established to last 2 sts, decrease once by working these 2 sts together in pattern — 56 (60, 64, 68) sts. Repeat this last row 4 more times — 48 (52, 56, 60) sts. **

Work even in pattern, without further shaping for 22 (24, 26, 28) rows, ending after a WS row.

Divide for Shoulders

Next Row: Work in pattern as established for 16 (18, 20, 20) sts for right shoulder, bind off in pattern next 16 (16, 16, 20) sts for Center Back, work in pattern as established across remaining 16 (18, 20, 20) sts for left shoulder. Place stitches for right shoulder on holder.

Left Shoulder

Working back and forth on sts of the left shoulder: Beginning with a WS row, work 2 rows in pattern as established.

Shape Neck

Row 1 (WS): Work in pattern to end of row.

Row 2: Decrease by working 2 sts together in pattern

at neck edge, work in pattern to end of row. Repeat last 2 rows twice more (all sizes), ending after RS row —13 (15, 17, 17) sts.

Work in pattern without shaping until Left Front shoulder is the same length as Left Back shoulder, ending with RS row.

Shape Shoulder

Row 1: (WS): Work in pattern to end of row.

Row 2: Work in pattern for 6 (7, 8, 8) sts, turn. Work in pattern to the end of the row at the neck edge. Break yarn and put these stitches on holder.

Right Shoulder

Transfer Right Shoulder sts from holder to circular needle.

Working back and forth on the sts of the right shoulder:

With the RS of the work facing you, join yarn at the armhole edge and work 3 rows in pattern as established.

Shape Neck

Row 1: (WS) Decrease once by working 2 sts together in pattern at neck edge, work in pattern to end of row.

Row 2: Work in pattern to end of row.

Repeat last 2 rows twice more — 13 (15, 17, 17) sts.

Shape Shoulder

Row 1: (WS): Work in pattern for 6 (7, 8, 8) sts, turn. Work in pattern to end of row at neck edge. Break yarn and put these sts on holder.

front

Transfer sts for Front from holder. Mark RS of Front with a safety pin, as a visual cue — 60 (64, 68, 72) sts.

Shape Armholes

Work as for Back from ** to **.

Work even in pattern without further shaping for 10 (12, 14 16) rows, ending with a WS row.

Divide for Shoulders

Next Row: (RS) Work in pattern for 16 (18, 20, 20) sts for left shoulder, bind off in pattern until 16 (18, 20, 20) sts remain unworked, including st remaining on right needle after binding off, work in pattern to end of row for right shoulder.

Place sts for left shoulder on holder.

Right Shoulder
Shape Neck

Rows 1–3: Work in pattern to end of row.

Row 4: Decrease in pattern by working 2 sts together in pattern at neck edge, work in pattern to end of row.

Repeat last 2 rows twice more — 13 (15, 17, 17) sts.

Work in pattern without shaping until Right Front Shoulder is the same length as Right Back shoulder, ending with a WS row.

Shape Shoulder

Row 1: (RS) Work in pattern for 6 (7, 8, 8) sts, turn. Work in pattern to end of row at neck edge. Break yarn. Place sts on holder.

Left Shoulder

Transfer left shoulder sts from holder to circular needle.

With RS of work facing, join yarn at armhole edge.

Shape Neck

Rows 1–3: Work in pattern.

Row 4: Work in pattern until 2 sts remain at neck edge, decrease by working these 2 sts together in pattern.

Repeat last 2 rows twice more — 13 (15, 17, 17) sts.

Shape Shoulder

Row 1: (WS) Work in pattern for 6 (7, 8, 8) sts, turn. Work in pattern to end of row at neck edge. Break yarn. Place sts on holder.

Join Shoulders

Turn garment inside out, so RS are facing each other. Place sts of Right Back shoulder and Right Front shoulder on two spare double pointed needles. With size 6 (4.0 mm) needle, work shoulders together using the 3-Needle Bind Off method.

Repeat for left shoulder.

finishing

Weave in ends, turn garment to RS, and block.

cuffs **first**

Here's something completely different — a jacket worked from cuff to center on both sides! Work your sweater in two pieces and join down the center back. This unusual construction also creates a back vent and, as you sew up the side seams, you can leave side vents as well. Have fun with different color combinations for the two sides or try a rainbow effect from cuff to cuff.

Style Notes: This is a knit only garment, worked vertically in Garter Stitch beginning at the cuffs. The Back is joined using a 3–Needle Bind Off. Some sewing required.

Designer: Deb Gemmell
Experience Level: Beginner

size
To fit Child: 1 (2, 4, 6)

finished measurements
Chest: 24 (26, 28, 30)"
Body Length: 12 (13, 15, 17)"
Sleeve Length: 6½ (8, 10, 12)"

materials
Chunky Weight Yarn (3.5 ounces/110 yards, 100 grams/101 meters per ball):
Light Blue or Blue (MC/Dark Color) 2 (2, 2, 2) balls
Cream or Gold (CC/Light Color) 2 (2, 2, 2) balls
Size 10 (6.0 mm) 24" (60 cm) circular needle
Stitch holder
Markers
Clasp(s)

gauge
14 sts = 4" (10 cm) on size 10 (6.0 mm) needle in Garter Stitch or size needed to obtain gauge

Cast on at the cuff and work the sleeve wider and wider for a dolman (batwing) sleeve. Cast on stitches to make up the length for the body and work to the Center Front and Back. Make a second side with another color and join the 2 sides at the Center Back.

Starting with the RS of the sweater and the Dark MC.

cuff

Begin with right side:

With circular needle and MC, cast on 25 (25, 29, 29) sts.

Row 1: (RS) Knit.

Row 2: K12 (12, 14, 14), place marker, P1, K12 (12, 14, 14) sts.

Row 3: Knit.

Row 4: Knit to marker, P1, knit to end of row.

Repeat Rows 3 and 4 until cuff measures 2½" from cast on edge.

sleeve

Increase Row: K2, M1, knit to last 2 sts, M1, K2.

Next Row: (WS) Knit to marker, P1, knit to end of row. Repeat last 2 rows until sleeve measures 6½ (8, 10, 12)" from cast on edge.

body

Next Row: Knit to marker, knit to end of row counting number of sts from marker to end of row. At end of row cast on number of stitches needed so that you have 41 (45, 53, 59) sts from marker to end of bind on.

Next Row: Knit 41 (45, 53, 59) sts to marker, P1, knit and count sts to end of row, at end of row cast on number of stitches needed so that you have 41 (45, 53, 59) sts from P1 stitch to end of cast on — 83 (91, 107, 119) sts on needle.

Stripe Pattern

Row 1: (RS) Knit.

Row 2: Knit to marker, P1, knit to end of row.

Continue to work 2 rows above, changing colors as follows:

2 rows CC.

2 rows MC.

Continue in stripes until body measures 3½ (4, 4½, 5)" from cast on for body. Cut MC.

With CC, work Rows 1 and 2 twice. **

Right Side Neck Opening

Next Row: (RS) K35 (39, 47, 53), cast off next 8 sts, knit to end of row.

back

Next Row: (WS) Knit first 40 (44, 52, 58) sts to bind off sts (Back).

Knit every row until Back measures 2" from bind off neck edge.

Back Vent: With WS facing, bind off first 8 sts of row, put 32 (36, 44, 50) remaining sts of Back onto stitch holder.

front

With WS facing, reattach CC at neck edge, K35 (39, 47, 53) sts of Front.

Knit every row for 2" to match the Back.

With RS facing, bind off while purling.

left side

With the CC, work as for RS to **.

Left Side Neck Opening

Next Row: (RS) K40 (44, 52, 58), bind off next 8 sts, knit to end of row.

front

Next Row: (WS) K35 (39, 47, 53) sts.

Knit every row for 2" from bind off neck edge.

With RS facing, bind off while purling.

back

Reattach MC to neck edge, K40 (44, 52, 58) sts.

Knit every row for 2" from bind off neck edge.

Back Vent: With RS facing, bind off first 8 sts.

Attach the 2 sides together at Center Back (several options):

1. Using 3-Needle Bind Off, hold Left Back and Right Back sts parallel with WS facing and cast off stitches on RS of sweater to make a ridge up the Center Back.

2. For a smooth seam down the Center Back, use 3-Needle Bind Off, hold Left Back and Right Back sts parallel with RS facing and bind off stitches on WS of sweater.

3. You can bind off both sides and sew a seam up the Center Back.

finishing

Sew in ends. Sew up sleeve seams and down the side seam of body, leaving a vent at the side seam, if desired.

Sew one clasp at the top of the Fronts. Sew on more clasps if desired.

resources

suppliers

BUTTONS (handmade):
Bull's Eye Button
PO Box 1416
Chautauqua, NY 14722
Phone (716) 357-2500 / Fax (716) 357-2515
All buttons are individually handcrafted of polymer clay. They are machine washable and may be put in the dryer on low. They should not be drycleaned. We recommend laundering your garment turned to the inside. All button designs are copyrighted and done in limited editions.

YARN:

Kraemer Yarns
www.kraemeryarns.com
PO Box 72, 240 South Main Street
Nazareth, PA 18064
Phone (800) 759-5601 / Fax (610) 759-4157
Little Lehigh and Lehigh Pebbles – both 45% cotton/55% acrylic machine washable.

S. R. Kertzer
www.kertzer.com
50 Trowers Road
Woodbridge, ON L4L 7K6 Canada
Phone (800) 263-2354 / (866) 444-1250
Butterfly Super 10 – machine wash and dry 100% cotton. DK.
Stylecraft Eskimo DK – 100% polyester, machine washable.
Wendy's Fashion Emu Superwash – 100% wool.

Cascade Yarns, Inc.
www.cascadeyarns.com
PO Box 58168
1224 Andover Park East
Tukwila, WA 98138
Phone (206) 574-0440
Cascade 220 Superwash – 100% wool.

Brown Sheep Company, Inc.
www.brownsheep.com
100662 County Road 16
Mitchell, Nebraska 69357
Phone (800) 826-9136 / Fax (308) 635-2143
Lamb's Pride Superwash – 100% machine washable wool. Bulky weight.

The Old Mill Knitting Company Inc.
www.oldmillknitting.com
F.G. PO Box 81176
Ancaster, Ontario L9G 4X2
Phone (905) 648-3483 / Fax (905) 648-1173
Naturally Buttons – machine washable 83% wool/17 polyester effect.
Naturally Tussock – hand wash, 85% wool/15% polyester effect.

Sweaterkits
www.sweaterkits.com
PO Box 397
Sharon, Ontario,
L0G 1V0, Canada
Toll free in Canada & USA:
Phone (877) 232-9415 / Fax (905) 898-3671
Cotton Licious – 100% cotton, machine washable.

yarns used in models

Sophia's Ridged Cardigan, Page 8
Kraemer Little Lehigh Yarn, Peek-a-boo,
Bull's Eye Buttons

Mariposa Blocks, Page 12
S. R. Kertzer Butterfly Super 10 Cotton Yarn,
Model 1: #3861 Indigo, #3856 Kelly Green,
#3997 Scarlet, #3533 Daffodil, #3871 Cobalt
Model 2: #3722 Teal, #3784 Tiger Lily Orange,
#3722 Pistachio, #3525 Cornsilk, #3882
Periwinkle, Bull's Eye Buttons

Dazzling Poncho & Bag, Page 18
Model 1: S. R. Kertzer Brown Sheep Bulky
Superwash Wool, SW01 Red Wing, Stylecraft
Eskimo Eyelash, #5172 Ebony
Model 2: Naturally Tussock, #572 Purple, S. R.
Kertzer Stylecraft Eskimo Eyelash #5244 Purple

Autumn Stripes, Page 28
Model 1: Brown Sheep Lamb's Pride Superwash
Bulky, SW145 Blaze, SW13 Corn Silk
Model 2: Brown Sheep Lamb's Pride Superwash
Bulky, SW130 Blueberry Sorbet, SW57
Cornflower

Princess Cables Tunic & Hat, Page 34
Model 1: Kraemer Little Lehigh Yarn, Rubber
Ducky (yellow).
Model 2: S. R. Kraemer Butterfly Super 10
Cotton, #3446 Shell Pink

Twisted Cables Pullover & Hat, Page 42
Model 1: S. R. Kertzer Wendy's Fashion Emu
Superwash Wool, #1527 Bluebell
Model 2: S. R. Kertzer Butterfly Super 10
Cotton, #3202 Linen

Top Down Ridges, Page 48
Cascade 220 Superwash, #851 Lime Green,
Bull's Eye Buttons

Daddy's Little Helper Jean Jacket, Page 54
Kraemer Little Lehigh Yarn, It's A Boy

The Cameron, Page 60
Cascade 220 Superwash, #813 Navy Blue, #851
Mint Green

Sam's Delight, Page 64
Cascade 220 Superwash, #809 Red, #813 Blue

Sherbet Stripes Hoodie Sweater, Page 68
Kraemer Little Lehigh Yarn, Baby Powder,
Rubber Ducky, Sleepyhead, Peek-a-boo, It's a
Boy
Kraemer Little Lehigh Pebbles Yarn, Playtime

Sassy Stripes Hoodie Vest, Page 74
Naturally Magic Garden Buttons, #6303 Cobalt
Blue, #6892 Emerald Green

La Petite Chanel, Page 80
S. R. Kertzer Butterfly Super 10 Mercerized
Cotton, #3346 Powder Pink, #3451 Blush,
Cream. Eyelash by S. R. Kertzer Baton Rouge
Eyelash, #2009 Tumbleweed

Little Boy Blue Striped Vest, Page 86
Cotton Licious from SweaterKits, #12 Navy, #05
Ocean, #03 Princess Purple

Northern Lights Sweater & Hat, Page 90
Cascade 220 Superwash wool, #809 Red, #813
Navy Blue, #851 Lime Green, #825 Orange

Pretty In Points Vest, Page 96
Cotton Licious from SweaterKits in
#15 Periwinkle, Bull's Eye Buttons

Pop Top, Page 100
Model 1: S. R. Kertzer Butterfly Super 10
cotton, #3995 Persian Red
Model 2: #3777 Seafoam

Cuff's First, Page 106
Brown Sheep Co. Lambs Pride Superwash Bulky
Model 1: SW10 Alabaster, SW130 Blueberry
Sorbet
Model 2: SW57 Cornflower, SW13 Corn Silk